D1483925

DARK GLORY

A Picture of the Church among
Negroes in the Rural South

by

HARRY V. RICHARDSON

Published for
Home Missions Council of North America
and
Phelps-Stokes Fund
by
Friendship Press - New York

HARRY V. RICHARDSON has for the past fourteen years been chaplain and director of religious activities at Tuskegee Institute in Alabama. At present he is executive secretary and field director of a Southwide program for the training of the Negro rural ministry—a program sponsored jointly by the Home Missions Council and the Phelps-Stokes Fund.

He is a native of Jacksonville, Florida, where he received his early education. He is a graduate of Western Reserve University in Cleveland, Ohio, and of the Harvard Divinity School, from which he graduated with honors. He received his Ph. D. degree at Drew University.

Under Dr. Richardson's ministry the Tuskegee Chapel has become one of the outstanding pulpits of the South. He is widely known as a leader of young people. He is a frequent contributor to leading publications.

Second Printing

TO

RALPH A. FELTON

WHOSE INTEREST IN
LIFTING SUPPRESSED PEOPLES
HAS BEEN AN INSPIRATION

CONTENTS

CONTENTS

TABLES

FOREWORD

It is generally agreed that the Negro church is the greatest institution developed by Negroes on American soil. It has held in common unity more Negroes than any other organization, and it has had more influence in molding the thought and life of the Negro people than any other single agency. The fact is often overlooked, however, that in its major development and until comparatively recent years, the Negro church was predominantly a rural church.

American Negro slavery underwent its most extensive growth with the development of cotton plantations in the South. It was on these plantations that the great majority of Negroes were found. It was on these plantations that the great majority of Negroes were converted to Christianity, and looked to it for whatever solace or service it had to offer a slave. It was on these plantations, both before the emancipation and after, that Negroes sought to worship God.

Human slavery is a terrible ordeal for any people who have to suffer it. It hurts the body and it hurts the soul. The fact that most Negroes were not more deeply injured by it is due in large part to the influence of the rural Negro church. The fact that a people forced to live in the moral and the physical filth of slave status could still aspire to the love and the beauty and the goodness of God is ineradicable witness of their spiritual greatness. The medium through which they expressed this greatness and the instrument that kept the impulse strong was the limited, humble, crude, but transcendently noble rural Negro church.

To be sure, the rural church is and has been open to criticism at many points. For one, its leaders have not always been men of highest caliber. But when all things are considered, this lack of adequate leadership is more a reflection on education than on the church. Negro theological education, like white education, has in the past made little effort to prepare men for service in the rural field. That is, it has neither trained nor inspired men to serve in an area of great need through an institution that is capable of rendering an enormous service.

It has often been said that the rural Negro church has not served as an instrument of protest. In this respect it is compared with other American Negro institutions. The charge that the church has not vigorously or consistently protested against conditions in the South is true. But the charge is often made without seeing the full picture of a lone leader working in the midst of violent, deadly repressive forces, charged with the responsibility of preserving his people who, like himself, are subject to the same destructive pressures. We know now that both the value and effect of a protest are dependent upon the nature of the conscience to which the protest is addressed. The Southern conscience on matters of race today, as in times past, is such as to make unbridled protest questionable, and to make discretion almost imperative in speaking the truth when the larger welfare of the people is involved.

The surplus of emotion, the lack of educated forms, the crude, homely worship of the rural church, are often pointed out in criticism. But again, while valid, the reflection falls elsewhere than on the church. No institution is better than its leaders, and good leaders in large numbers have not been trained to serve the rural church. It has been left in the main to men of lesser gifts, and it reflects all the weaknesses of this desertion. It can be said, too, that not all of the church is unwholesomely emotional, and that much of its emotionality is a hangover from the forms in which Christianity first came to the Negro convert.

When rounded consideration is given to the rural church, it is clear that it stands as the greatest institutional development of Negroes in America.

At the present time Negro life in the South is undergoing tremendous change. Migration, changes in agriculture, farm programs by state and federal agencies all are having their effect on the people, and consequently on the rural church. It is to show how deeply these various changes have affected the church that the present work is undertaken.

But there is a second motive, too. It sometimes happens that a part is an epitome of the whole. The rural Negro church is such a fragment. Carefully studied, it affords a fair picture of contemporary Christianity in rural America.

For example, in the rural Negro church is to be seen the queer disregard with which American Protestantism views the rural part of itself—the part that is strongest in faith and loyalty, and that provides replenishment for the constantly dwindling urban part. In the rural Negro church is to be seen the dichotomy of thought that splits our religion into black and white, thus violating our sense of Christian brotherhood and vitiating the power of the gospel that we preach. In the rural Negro church is to be seen the deliberate neglect of an area of great need, perhaps, unfortunately, because service in the area affords neither large sums of money nor great fame. As far as Negroes themselves are concerned, we see in the rural Negro church the weakness, the tragedy, of a great institution deserted by its leading minds. In short, in this neglected, backyard fragment of the Christian church, we see much of what contemporary American Protestantism is doing, what it is not doing, and what it needs to do.

While there have been several studies of the Negro church as a whole, there has been to date no full length study devoted solely to the rural Negro church. In the effort to meet this need it is hoped that the present work will prove useful.

Many persons generously assisted in the studies underlying this book. Especial gratitude is due to the Reverends N. M. Carter of Selma University; James S. Thomas of South Carolina State College; M. N. DeLaney of Arkansas Agricultural, Mechanical, and Normal College; H. C. Roane and H. M. Ruffin of Northumberland County, for assistance in making the field studies. County agents S. W. Boynton and U. P. Grigsby, and Mr. Edward Williams of the United States Department of Agriculture, were also most helpful. I am indebted to Professor Ralph A. Felton of Drew University for many useful suggestions.

H. V. R.

Tuskegee Institute, Alabama
January 1, 1947

Chapter One

HISTORICAL BACKGROUND

Early Attempts at Slave Conversion

Although from the beginning some effort was made to convert American Negro slaves to Christianity, for the first hundred years the effort was involved in controversy, and was therefore neither widespread nor very effective. The first slaves arrived at Jamestown, Virginia, in the year 1619. At that time, however, the idea was prevalent that one Christian should not hold another Christian in bondage. Consequently, upon becoming Christian a slave should also have become free. This naturally was a problem for those who had invested in slaves, and it led to much of the opposition that early missionaries faced in their work.

To settle the issue in Virginia the legislature of that colony declared in 1667 that baptism did not alter the condition of a person as to his bondage or freedom.

This started a process of enactments and rulings that removed the Christian religion as a legal barrier to slavery in the Colonies. In 1729 the Crown Attorney and Solicitor General ruled that baptism in no way changed a slave's legal status.[1] Two years previously the Bishop of London had declared:

> . . . Christianity does not make the least alteration in civil property; that the freedom which Christianity gives, is a freedom from the bondage of sin and Satan, and from the dominion of their lusts and passions and inordinate desires; but as to their outward condition they remained as before, even after baptism.

As the principle became established that conversion did not alter slave status, ministers and missionaries were freer to work among the slaves. The religious body that most actively undertook this work in the seventeenth and early eighteenth centuries was the Church of England through its Society for the Propagation of the Gospel in Foreign Parts. Since the Anglican Church was the major religious body in the Colonies, the responsibility of winning converts to Christianity fell mainly upon the ministers of this church. However, for many reasons they were not able to devote adequate effort to the task. To assist in evangelizing the growing colonial population the Society for the Propagation of the Gospel was organized in 1701. Its specific duties were: "the care and instruction of our people settled in the colonies; the conversion of the Indian savages, and the conversion of the Negroes."

Other bodies were active in the colonial period, but on a much smaller scale. Chief among them were the Moravian Brethren, the Presbyterians, and the Society of Friends. The Friends took the most positive stand against slavery of any of the religious bodies during this period. They alone made the possession of slaves a cause for expulsion from the church.

[1] *The Negro Church*, by W. E. B. DuBois, p. 10. Atlanta, Georgia, the Atlanta University Press, 1903.

It is the opinion of Marcus W. Jernigan, a student of Colonial history, that prior to the American Revolution, comparatively few slaves were converted to Christianity. His reasons as summarized from a published discussion of the subject are:

1. Masters feared that conversion would interfere with slave labor. Slaves were required to work on Sundays, which conflicted with Christian teaching, and further, when converted, slaves would be equal in one respect to their masters, which would make them harder to control.

2. The general interest in religion was low in Colonial times. Masters were not much interested in their own spiritual welfare, and consequently were not deeply concerned about the welfare of their slaves.

3. Many slaves were unable to understand religious teachings, due in large part to their lack of knowledge of the English language.

4. The slave's environment was not conducive to the Christian life.

5. The sparsely settled country and the difficulties of travel made it hard for ministers to serve their members, to say nothing of evangelizing the unchurched.[1]

It was not until the latter half of the eighteenth century, around the time of the American Revolution, that a number of significant developments took place that did much to spread Christianity among the slaves and to shape the course of Negro religion in America.

[1] Summary of statements from "Slavery and Conversion in the American Colonies," by Marcus W. Jernigan, in *American Historical Review*, Vol. XXI, No. 3 (April, 1916). Used by permission.

1. THE INFLUENCE OF COTTON

First of these developments was the increased production of cotton in response to a rapidly rising world demand. A series of remarkable inventions, beginning with the spinning and weaving machines in England and culminating in Whitney's cotton gin in America, greatly increased the output of cotton goods. The soil of the Southern colonies was admirably suited to grow the necessary cotton if an adequate supply of labor could be obtained. This labor was found in African Negro slaves, who first were legally imported into the country, then illegally smuggled, and all the while bred to meet the great demand. In 1790 there were approximately seven hundred thousand slaves in the United States. In 1860 there were four million. Over three million were in twelve Southern states, engaged for the most part in producing the cotton and other crops that were rapidly building up the fortunes of the wealthier group among the Southern planters.

This concentration of Negroes on the farms of the South meant that Christianity among them became predominantly a rural religion, or more accurately, the religion of a rural people. Thus the Negro church, like the white church, was in its major development a rural institution.

2. THE EVANGELICALS AND THE SLAVE

The second great development in Negro religion was the coming of the evangelical Christian bodies, particularly the Methodists, Baptists, and Presbyterians. These groups in their zeal to evangelize the young America, gave much attention to the growing body of slaves. In the early stage they were strongly abolitionist. They felt that slavery was wrong, and they openly preached against it. Freeborn Garretson said in 1776:

It was God, not man, that taught me the impropriety of holding slaves: and I shall never be able to praise him enough for it. My very heart has bled since that for slaveholders, especially those who make a profession of religion; for I believe it to be a crying sin.[1]

Bishop Asbury records in his Journal in 1780: "This I know. God will plead the cause of the oppressed though it gives offense to say so here. . . . I am grieved for slavery and the manner of keeping these poor people."[2]

Many preachers followed their words by freeing slaves they already held, and by refusing to become slaveholders. In 1780 the Methodists required all traveling preachers to set their slaves free. The Baptists, because of their policy of local church government, were not as uniform or as effective in their attack on slavery as the Methodists. Yet in 1789 a Baptist Convention declared:

Slavery is a violent depredation of the rights of nature and inconsistent with a republican government, and therefore, [we] recommend it to our brethren, to make use of their local missions to extirpate this horrid evil from the land; and pray Almighty God that our honorable legislature may have it in their power to proclaim the great jubilee consistent with the principles of good policy.[3]

Although the evangelicals found it necessary to retreat considerably from the high ground they first had taken against

---

[1] *History of the Negro Church*, by Carter G. Woodson, p. 28. Washington, D. C., the Associated Publishers, 1921. Used by permission.

[2] *Journal of Reverend Francis Asbury*, Vol. I, p. 306. New York, Lane and Scott, 1852.

[3] Woodson, *op. cit.*, p. 32.

slavery, they continued their efforts to convert the slaves, and to plead in the name of Christianity for amelioration of the more brutal aspects of slavery.

In seeking converts, the evangelicals had one great advantage over the Anglicans and other early missionaries. The evangelical religion was simple, personal, and only slightly ritualistic. It was ideally suited to the unlettered masses of the colonial frontier both white and black. In order to become an Anglican it was necessary to know the creed, the catechism, and other articles of faith, as well as to be able to follow the ritual of the service. To become a Methodist or Baptist it was only necessary to repent and accept Christ as personal Savior. This was a religion even the field-hand slave could understand. In the early evangelistic drives such as the Great Awakening and the Great Revival, large numbers of Negroes were converted. But if the simplicity of the evangelical faith did much to determine the number of Negroes who became Christians, the emotionalism of the early evangelical faith did much to determine the nature of Negro worship. The religion that the Negro masses first received was characterized by such phenomena as laughing, weeping, shouting, dancing, barking, jerking, prostration, and speaking in tongues. These were regarded as evidence of the Spirit at work in the heart of man, and they were also taken as evidence of the depth and sincerity of the conversion. It was inevitable, therefore, that early Negro worship should be filled with these emotional elements.

Although there is some tendency to regard high emotionalism as a phenomenon peculiar to the Negro church, in reality it is a hangover from the days of frontier religion. It should also be said that emotionalism of this type is to be found to-day chiefly among the less cultured rural and urban churches.[1]

3. THE NEGRO PREACHER

The third development that did much to shape the course of Negro religion was the rise of Negro preachers. These leaders began to appear in the latter part of the eighteenth century, the time when large numbers of Negroes were being converted to Christianity. Prominent among them were Black Harry (c. 1782), who traveled with Bishop Asbury and was a great attraction; David George (c. 1775), preacher of the first Negro Baptist church at Silver Bluff, South Carolina; George Liele, of Burke County, Georgia, an eloquent preacher to blacks and whites; Andrew Bryan of Georgia (1737-1812), founder of the First African Baptist Church of Savannah; John Chavis (c. 1801) who was made a missionary to slaves by the Presbyterians; and Henry Evans, organizer of the white Methodist church at Fayetteville, North Carolina, in 1790.[2] Most unusual among these early preachers was Lemuel Haynes, 1753-1833, a mulatto of learning and eloquence who through all of his ministry pastored only white Congregational churches in New England. He was quite a theologian, and debated with power the theological issues of his time.

The Negro preacher played a significant part in the social and religious development of Negro life. First, preaching was an outlet for leadership ability. It was the one position of leadership permitted Negroes, and the office carried consider-

[1] *An American Dilemma,* by Gunnar Myrdal, Vol. II, pp. 937-8. New York, Harper and Brothers, 1944.
[2] Woodson, *op. cit.,* Chapter III.

able prestige. It did much to keep aspiration alive among gifted Negro men. Secondly, the Negro preacher was able to communicate religion to the slave in a useful and intimate form. Being one of the people and suffering with them, he could make religion not only a discipline but also a living ground of hope.

The preachers' task was hard, however. While preaching to slaves, they could not attack slavery. Many had been granted the privilege of preaching and the liberties that went with it through the kindness of masters who trusted them. To have attacked the slave system would have meant violating this trust. Also, since the controls over the slaves were so rigid and severe, it may easily have meant exciting the people to no advantage at the cost of terrible penalties.

The role of the Negro slave preacher seems typified in this description of George Liele:

The unusual tact of George Liele was the key to his success. He seemed to know how to handle men diplomatically, but some of his policy may be subject to criticism. Unlike so many Baptist and Methodist missionaries who came forward preaching freedom of body and soul to all men and thereby stirring up the slaves in certain parts, George Liele would not receive any slaves who did not have permission of their owners, and instead of directing attention to their wrongs, conveyed to them the mere message of Christ. His influence among the masters and overseers became unusual, and the membership of his church rapidly increased. No literature was used, and no instruction given, until it had first been shown to the members of the legislature, the magistrates, and the justices to secure their permission beforehand. One of the masters, speaking of the wholesome influence of Liele's preaching, said that he did not need to employ an assistant nor to make use of the whip whether he was at home or elsewhere, as his slaves were industrious and obedient, and lived together in unity, brotherly love, and peace.[1]

Not all the Negro preachers were as tactful or as submissive as Liele. One white Methodist minister of the South Carolina Conference complained that Negro preachers wanted all the rights and opportunities of white preachers. Also, Nat Turner, leader of the slave rebellion of 1831, was a self-styled preacher.[2]

Types of Slave Churches

There were three distinct types of churches in the time of slavery: the mixed church, the separate church under white leadership, and the separate church under Negro leadership. As Johnson and Johnson point out, all three types existed simultaneously, but the gradual tendency was toward the separate, all-Negro church.[3]

1. THE MIXED CHURCH

In many cases when Negroes were converted they were accepted into membership in the white church. As a rule, and especially in the South, separate seating space was provided for them, such as the balcony of the church or the back pews. This mixed membership persisted in many churches down to the Emancipation and even into the Reconstruction period.

A modified form of the mixed church was that in which

[1] Woodson, *op. cit.*, p. 47. Used by permission.

[2] DuBois, *op. cit.*, pp. 22-26.

[3] *The Church and the Race Problem,* by Guy B. Johnson and Guion G. Johnson, Vol. II, p. 240. Unpublished manuscript prepared for the Carnegie Study, 1940. Schomburg collection, Harlem Branch of the New York Public Library.

Negroes were listed as members of a white church but worshiped in separate services. Marie Clare Boyd writes of one such church in Alabama:

The presence of the colored members is often apparent in the minutes of the New Cubahatchee Church. In that church they were met in conferences separately, and the state of fellowship and order investigated. They dealt with such cases as that of the slave, Lucy, who was living in a disorderly and disgraceful manner. The church did much to maintain order and decency among the Negroes.[1]

The mixed church was faced with a number of difficulties, social as well as religious. Masters hesitated to enter into the intimacies of church fellowship with their slaves; preaching suited to the master was often considered wrong for the slave; masters were hesitant to give vent to their emotions before their slaves, and slaves in turn were inhibited in the presence of their masters.

2. THE SEPARATE CHURCH UNDER WHITE LEADERSHIP

Many of these difficulties were solved in the separate church or mission presided over by a white pastor, who was generally regarded as a missionary to the Negroes. It avoided social mixing, it permitted special preaching to slaves, and it provided the one element about which there was so much uneasiness, white supervision of Negro gatherings. Something of these separate churches is seen in a passage from T. M. Owen's history of Alabama:

. . . The Baptist State Convention of 1844 recognized the duty

[1] *Alabama in the Fifties,* by Marie Clare Boyd, p. 167. New York, Columbia University Press, 1931. Used by permission.

of using all practicable and legal means of instructing slaves in the Christian religion.

Preachers were urged, with the consent of masters, to "assemble the colored people, in no very great numbers at one time or place, on the plantations or at the churches, as may be convenient, and adapt discourses especially to them; that they pray and sing with them and endeavor to guide them into the way of heaven."

Members of churches were urged to erect suitable houses of worship on the plantations or in some convenient situations, with the proviso "not to produce annoyance to the neighbors, or lead into temptation by the assemblage of large numbers of them together, or far from their home."[1]

The chief difficulty with the separate church under white leadership was that there were not enough white ministers to undertake the task of evangelizing the vast number of slaves.

3. THE SEPARATE CHURCH UNDER NEGRO LEADERSHIP

A separate church led by Negroes could have solved all the problems of slave church life, except for the fact that this type was in itself a problem. A meeting of Negroes led by Negroes was always a potential source of rebellion or trouble. Although tolerated by the whites, they were not generally encouraged and always they were carefully watched. The slave rebellions under Denmark Vesey and Nat Turner increased the disfavor of the separate, all-Negro church.

Yet the number of independent churches steadily increased. Some of the first churches among Negroes have been previously mentioned. In 1821 an African Baptist church was established at Huntsville, Alabama. No accurate figures are available, but it is known that practically all of the Southern states had some

[1] *History of Alabama and Dictionary of Alabama Biography,* by Thomas N. Owen, Vol. II, p. 180. Chicago, S. J. Clark Publishing Co., 1921.

of these all-Negro churches by the time of the Civil War.[1]

In almost every instance these churches were Baptist. A Baptist church is a local organization. This made it possible for the whites to know the membership and the leaders, and to control the policies of the church. With Baptist churches there would be no national connections with policies differing from those of the immediate community, and there would be no visiting officials with undesirable ideas. Furthermore, the extensive traveling characteristic of the Methodist itinerancy was not possible for either a slave or a free Negro in the South. Because of these obstacles of church practice and policy Negro Methodist bodies did not become established in the South prior to the emancipation.

The African Methodist Episcopal Church, one of the earliest Negro denominations, made a single attempt to maintain a church at Charleston, South Carolina, but in 1822, a year after Denmark Vesey's abortive rebellion, the church was broken up, its minister was attacked and forced to flee the community, and the effort of this body to work in the South had to be abandoned.

The Emancipation and After

On September 22, 1862, President Lincoln issued the Declaration of Emancipation that was to become effective January 1, 1863. Although it was not immediately enforcible in many parts of the South since unoccupied sections were outside the control of the national government, freedom became a reality for all Negroes with the close of the Civil War. Thenceforth they were free to move and to organize as they wished.

[1] Woodson, *op. cit.*, Chapter V.

[12]

The great mass of undeveloped, unchristianized freemen in the South presented opportunity for many kinds of humanitarian service. Along with philanthropic whites who came into the South to render educational as well as religious aid to the freemen, Negro missionaries also came as representatives of independent Negro denominations, seeking to win members for their particular churches from among the former slaves.

Partly because of their racial appeal, partly because of their greater activity, the Negro workers won far more members than the representatives of the white church bodies. In fact, the early days of the Reconstruction were marked by a strong tendency toward independent, all-Negro religious organizations. In the decade between 1860 and 1870 the African Methodist Episcopal Zion Church, one of the two principal Negro Methodist bodies, grew from 26,746 members to 200,000. The African Methodist Episcopal Church, the other leading Negro Methodist group, in 1880 claimed a membership of 400,000. For both churches most of their members were the freemen in the rural South.

Baptists continued as the most numerous group among Negroes in the South. In this church, as in the Methodist, the tendency was toward independent, all-Negro units. Even in cases where Negroes had been members of white churches on amicable terms, there still was a desire for the separate all-colored church. An excellent illustration is found in the origin of Shiloh Baptist Church, Northumberland County, Virginia. In 1867 the 38 colored members of Fairfield Baptist Church (white) addressed the following petition to the white members:

Poplar Stage, July 7, 1867

To Elder William Kirk and the Members of the
Fairfield Baptist Church:

Beloved Brothers: Grace be unto you and peace from God, the father of our Lord Jesus Christ. From an earnest desire to act in all things with an eye single to the glory of God and for the unity of that common faith which constitute us in Christ Jesus, we have thought it advisable to counsel on the subject of our future church relation. So that whatever may be done we may at least preserve that peace and harmony which ought to characterize those of the same faith and order and promote the prosperity of that cause which, through your instrumentality, had been the means of calling us into the light and knowledge of the glorious gospel of the Son of God. Without alluding to the Providence that so mysteriously changed our social and political relation, we conceive that under the new order of things we are not only advanced in our religious privilege, but that solemn and weighty responsibilities impose upon us a new class of duties in which we should be wanting in fidelity if we did not seek to place ourselves in that position in which we could best promote our mutual good, both in reference to ourselves and our posterity. In this new relation the subject of a separate church organization presses itself upon us as the best possible way in which we can best promote those indispensable interests, such as an ordained ministry, a separate congregation with all the privileges of a church organization, stated church meetings, regular religious service, Sabbath schools, etc. But just at this point the question arises: Can we not do this and preserve the unity of the faith and continue in church fellowship with our white brethren; and thereby perpetuate our church identity, so that in all the general interest of the church we may be mutually interested and to some extent co-laborers? To effect this may require the concurrent action of all the members of the congregation concerned; and the object of this communication is to ask your attention to this subject with the hope that such an arrangement can be made as to induce a general church meeting at some convenient time and place for this purpose, that our identity may be preserved or perpetuated if possible; and if not, that we may receive your parting benediction and blessing, as well as your endonation [endorsement] of our Christian character and standing. All of which is most respectfully submitted for your prayerful consideration and action. Hoping that unerring wisdom may guide us in the way of all truth, we remain, dear brethren in the bonds of Christ.

> Yours Fraternally,
> SAMUEL CONWAY, Secretary
> HIRMAN KENNER, Chairman[1]

The letter was received by the white members in their regular church meeting, August 10, 1867, and the petition was unanimously granted. Two white members donated small plots of land on which a temporary place of worship was erected for the new congregation.

The Negro Church Today[2]

The most recent United States Census of Religious Bodies shows that in 1936 there were 38,303 Negro churches in this country, with a total membership of 5,660,618. Of the 38,303 churches, 13,528 were urban, while 24,775 were rural. Thus the rural churches outnumbered the urban almost two to one. In membership, however, the rural church was about a quarter of a million under the urban church. Of the 5,660,618 members, 2,958,630 were urban, while 2,701,988 were rural.

[1] *The Negro Church in Rural Virginia,* by C. H. Hamilton and John M. Ellison. Bulletin No. 273, Virginia Agricultural Experiment Station, 1930. Used by permission.

[2] As used in this work, the term Negro church includes all congregations whose members are wholly composed of Negroes, even congregations that are part of white denominations.

The Negro church is predominantly Southern, and a majority of the Southern members are rural. In fourteen Southern states there were 32,468 churches with a membership of 4,559,496. Of this number 2,598,542, or 57 per cent, were rural in 1936.

In rural sections, as in the nation, Baptists constituted a majority of the Negro church, something over two-thirds. Of the 24,775 rural churches, 16,385 were Baptist; Methodists were second with 6,182 rural Methodist churches. In rural membership, Baptists numbered 1,949,353, out of the total of 2,701,988. Methodists had 661,990 rural members.

Chapter Two

THE GENERAL SETTING

Any fair appraisal of the work of a church must take into account the locale in which the church labors, for the greatness or weakness of a church is determined by the way it meets the needs of its particular environment. In the case of the rural Negro church the locale is the South. Practically all rural churches among Negroes are located in this section.

It is customary to think and speak of the South as though it were a geographical and human unit, yet in reality it is neither. It is a highly varied region whose many component elements differ markedly from one another in history, in economic patterns, in cultural and social behavior. Thus in general terms it is possible to speak of the Upper South, such states for example as Virginia, North Carolina, and Kentucky, with their farmstead pattern of agriculture, their smaller proportion of Negroes, and as far as Negroes are concerned, somewhat higher standards of living. In these respects the Upper South differs sharply from the Lower South, such states for example as Georgia and Mississippi, with their plantation pattern of agriculture, their larger number of Negroes, and as far as Negroes are concerned, more severe repressions and lower standards of living.

In order, therefore, that the picture of the South as the setting of the rural church should be representative of the South's varied regions, four counties in different sections were selected for special study. They were Dallas County in Alabama, representative of the South Central section, a region now undergoing extensive agricultural change; Calhoun County in South Carolina, representative of the Lower Piedmont region of the Southeast; Mississippi County in Arkansas, representative of the West South Central section and the Mississippi Delta, a county of racially mixed tenantry; and Northumberland County in Virginia, representative of the Upper South.

In choosing counties as units for study it was recognized that county lines are not natural boundaries for rural pastorates. Many ministers have churches in two or more counties, and Methodist circuits often run through two counties or more. Yet a county is the handiest administrative unit for which extensive statistics are available, and chiefly for this reason the county was chosen.

The Rural South—A General View

Living conditions among Negroes in the rural South have been the object of careful, factual study for many years, especially since the beginning of the present century. In fact, these conditions have been so frequently studied and so widely publicized that they are now nationally notorious.

Some of the more significant studies are listed in the reading list on page 194. From these studies a few general conclusions may be set forth briefly, particularly as pertaining to the lower South. All are agreed that in every area of life Negroes in the rural South live on a level below the standard of Southern whites, which is itself below the national standard. For example, the income of the average Negro farm family in the South is much lower than that of the white. This is true on every agricultural level from sharecropper to owner. The income of Negroes in Southern villages is also much lower than that of whites. In the Consumer Purchases Study of 1935 it was found that while the median annual income of the white families studied was $1,200, the income of corresponding Negro families was only $300.

In housing the disparity is equally great. Southern rural housing is generally below the national standard. Of five and a half million rural homes, less than three million have water within fifty feet; four million have outside toilets or privies, and 657,799 have no toilets or privies at all. Yet for Negroes the record is lower still. In eleven Southern states it was found that one-fourth of Negro homes were unfit for habitation, and half of the remainder had poor foundations, poor roofs, and poor interiors. Only about one-fourth of the houses had screens, and these were often in poor condition.

Worst of all, perhaps, is the Southern Negro diet. In a recent survey it was found that one-third of the families studied consumed either none or very small quantities of milk and eggs. Fresh fruit was wholly lacking in the diet of two-thirds of these families. Such facts have led one writer to conclude that a majority of the Negro population suffers from severe malnutrition.

As to health and health services, the state of Arkansas has

1.4 hospital beds for each thousand of the white population, but only 0.9 for each thousand Negroes. In the South the mortality of white mothers per 1,000 live births is 2; among Negro mothers it is 5.5. In the South Negroes suffer to a much greater extent than whites from malaria, tuberculosis, and the venereal diseases. Yet the state of Mississippi has but five public health nurses for a population of a million Negroes, a population that is predominantly rural and poor. It is little wonder then that the Negro mortality rate in the South is 30 to 40 per cent higher than that of whites, and the life expectancy ten to twelve years shorter.

The inequalities in Southern public education have recently received wide publicity. In one Southern county, for example, of 11 Negro school buildings, one is brick, 10 are wooden. Of the 27 white school buildings in the same county, 23 are brick and 4 are wooden structures. All of the white schools have inside running water, janitor service, and a central heating plant. None of the Negro schools has inside water, all are heated by stoves in the open rooms, and teachers and students must do their own janitor work. It should be said, however, that at the present time many Southern states are making serious efforts to improve conditions among Negro schools. Negro education is one of the areas in which greatest current progress is being made.

Recreational and cultural facilities such as parks, playgrounds, and public libraries for whites in the rural South are woefully inadequate. For Negroes they are almost nonexistent.

In summary it may be said that at the present time, as far as Negroes are concerned, the rural South is a region of inequalities, disadvantages, and serious problems. And added to all this is the fact that throughout the region Negroes are widely disfranchised and have little part in civic affairs. And most ironic, the police and the courts, which ought to be sources of protection, in some Southern sections actually become further sources of trouble and persecution.

The conditions depicted here obtain generally throughout the Lower South. They are a little better in some ways in the Upper South as the study of Northumberland County in Virginia will show.

Four Selected Counties

I. DALLAS COUNTY, ALABAMA

Dallas County was chosen for study because it is in the heart of a Southern area that is undergoing radical agricultural change. The county is fairly large, 985 square miles, with a population in 1940 of 55,245, of which Negroes number 40,744 or 73.8 per cent. There is but one city, Selma, with a population of 19,834, but small villages are numerous throughout the county.

The county's agricultural history goes back to about 1818, the end of open warfare with the Creeks and Cherokees. Earliest settlers came from Virginia, North and South Carolina, Georgia, and Tennessee, and rapidly took up the more desirable lands, often in enormous tracts. Cotton soon became the principal cash crop, and in order to clear the land for it, vast stands of rich virgin timber were destroyed. With cotton, of course, came the slave and the plantation system. Since the Civil War the large tracts have been broken up into smaller farms that now are rented out to tenants. In 1935 it was found that 86.2 per cent of the farms in the county were tenant operated.

The principal agricultural development in the county is the change from cotton to cattle. A recent study shows that while cotton acreage in Dallas County declined from 153,000 acres in 1929 to 51,000 in 1939, beef cattle production increased from 3,700 in 1930 to 8,900 in 1940. The change is highly significant for the Negroes living in the areas affected. A decrease of 7 per cent in the Negro population of the county was observed in the sixteenth United States Census, 1940, and this was before the war had accelerated the rural-to-urban migration. This decline, it is believed, will be permanent for two reasons:

1. The type of farming in the Black Belt area is shifting more and more to beef cattle production—an extensive type of farming. Fewer people will find employment on the farms of the area.

2. Increased use of farm machinery and consequently greater efficiency in production will decrease the number of persons to be employed on the farms in the area. The number of farm boys who remain on the farm is closely related to the number of farms that have financial returns comparable with the pay they are able to get in other vocations.[1]

The way the change affects the individual Negro farmer on the soil may be glimpsed from field notes made during the study:

Informant: Mr. G—— P——.
He has farmed in this area all his adult life. He now rents 25 acres on which he grows cotton, cane, corn, and food crops. As a

[1] Cf. "Basic Facts on the Agriculture of the Black Belt Type-of-Farming Area Designed to Establish Sound Bases for Program Planning in the Black Belt Counties," by J. R. Otis, pp. 2, 18, 26. Tuskegee Institute, Alabama, 1944. Used by permission.

rule he "comes out" at the end of the year (that is, free of debt), but his earnings are small. He lives comparatively well, has a milk cow and calf, chickens, turkeys, one mule.

His farm is in the midst of a large tract entirely devoted to pasture for beef cattle. He feels his landlord allows him to hold his plot largely out of sentiment. His landlord formerly grew cotton, but has now changed to cattle.

Mr. P—— has not yet had to move, but expects to at any time. He has no living children, and no relatives to whom he can go. Yet he has not a single plan for the future and apparently little concern. His passivity is surprising.

He believes the present displacement of Negroes is nothing to what will come. In the next one or two years he thinks only cattle will be raised.

He believes, however, that someday Negroes will be re-established on the land. He stated: "I won't be here to see it, but somebody will see it. We will get the land again."

His wife is in poor health, and seems much more worried about the fate facing them than her husband.

Informant: Mr. S—— W——.

"A landlord can get as much for a steer as he can make on a Negro tenant in a year. He can raise twenty-five cows where he keeps one Negro. That's why they tell you: 'I'd rather see a white-faced bull on my land than to see a black-faced Negro.'"

In general, Negro life in the county is characteristic of tenant areas. Illiteracy is high, 33.7 per cent for Negroes as compared with 0.9 for whites, and 24.9 for the total population of the county. Similarly, expenditures for education are unequally distributed: $56.65 per white child, $13.45 per colored. Only 5.4 per cent of the Negro farmers are owners. Much of the land owned by Negroes is in the hilly, sandy sections.

Most of the white owners live in the small towns or in the

city and rent out the land to Negro tenants. This means, therefore, that many communities in the country are predominantly, sometimes wholly, made up of Negroes. These all-Negro villages, however, show little difference from the colored sections of mixed towns. They have no more business or civic or social developments than one would find in a mixed town. They prove clearly that segregation in itself is no virtue, and that progress is only possible when people possess basic economic and cultural opportunities.

Sometimes in these all-Negro communities a large proportion of the colored people own their homes. But again these owner communities have the same appearance as those in which most Negroes are renters. While the houses are larger than most tenant cabins, they still are almost always run down and in disrepair. One ready explanation for this condition is lack of interest in property maintenance and lack of community leadership. The more basic reason, however, is that the Negro owner in some rural sections has little more economic freedom than the tenant, especially in his efforts to market produce and get credit.

Racial Atmosphere

The relations between the races in Dallas County are the bewildering medley that race relations in the South so often become. They present the queer contrast between overt oppression on the one hand, and hopeful, though weak, goodwill on the other.

Most of the ministers said relations were "good," which, as shown in Chapter Nine, means mainly that there had been no recent violence. While there had not been any open clashes between racial groups, reliable accounts were heard of most unjustifiable brutality by police officers and citizens. Such accounts, for instance, told of the cruel beating of a colored woman by two white men as a policeman supervised the beating, because she had refused to carry out an insulting errand; and of the beating of a returned Negro army flyer by a group of leading citizens because he had refused to say "Yes, Ma'am" to a white woman clerk at a gasoline ration board. The air was thick with rumors that whites were secretly arming in preparation for trouble in the post-war period, particularly when the Negro soldiers returned with ideas of equality gained overseas. It was undoubtedly true that Negroes could not buy firearms or ammunition of any kind, not even shot-gun shells for hunting. Yet colored porters in stores said that arms and ammunition were sold readily to whites.

Rumors and stories such as these kept the racial atmosphere of the county tense and, for Negroes, suppressive. Between 1901 and 1931 Dallas County had five lynchings. According to a number of informed county residents, as sentiment against lynching grows in the South, killing and maltreatment of persons suspected of crime are now done by police officers under the excuse of "resisting arrest" or "attempting to escape."

This is a general picture of life in the county, but it does not account for the many exceptions that often were in direct contrast to the general picture. For example, in one community, a Negro and a white landlord whose plantations adjoined were the best of friends, and together "ran" the community. The treatment of tenants on one plantation was the same as that on the other. The Negro landlord "bossed" his church as the white landlord "bossed" his. A militant, rebellious pastor lasted no longer in one church than in the other. Or again, in this county the doctrine of absolute separation of the races is talked. But a number of most intimate relationships between the races was found, ranging all the way from perfectly wholesome friendships and business associations at one end, to illicit sexual commingling at the other. The effect of the racial situation was well phrased by one informant: "It's the fact that you never know what to expect that keeps you worried to death."

2. CALHOUN COUNTY, SOUTH CAROLINA

Calhoun County, named for John C. Calhoun, is located in the central part of the state of South Carolina. It is a small county of 391 square miles. It has three distinct soil types: the coastal plain type in the southern and southeast section; a strip of piedmont (gravel) soil seven miles wide running southeasterly across the central section; and the sandhill type in the north and west sections of the county.

The first white settlers were colonists who came from the northern part of Europe, beginning as early as 1732. The county has no large towns. St. Matthews with a population of 1,750 is the largest, and the county seat. It is almost wholly a rural-farm area. Cotton is the main crop. Others are corn, oats, soybeans, potatoes (Irish and sweet), peas, peanuts, asparagus, and pecans.[1] In 1940 Negroes constituted 73.1 per cent of the county's population of 16,229.

[1] *South Carolina, A Handbook,* prepared by the South Carolina Department of Agriculture, Commerce and Industries and Clemson College, Columbia, South Carolina, 1927.

There are a number of large plantations in the county, although most of the land is in farms rented to Negroes. Negro farm ownership is low, but somewhat higher than in Dallas County, 7.4 per cent. Living conditions in this county appear to be about the same as those in Dallas County. Illiteracy is high, 21.1 per cent for Negroes as compared with 1.0 per cent for whites. Expenditures for education are unequal, $72.82 per white pupil as compared with $17.54 per colored. Life on the plantations is typical of plantation life elsewhere: poor housing, low income, small opportunity. Incidentally, this is the county about which Julia Peterkin has written romantically in *Scarlet Sister Mary* and *Roll, Jordan, Roll*.

Racial Atmosphere

Racial conditions in this county are about the same as for Dallas and Mississippi counties, except that here the Negroes seemed more timid and suppressed. Some insight into the condition may be gained from the two following incidents.

In 1934 a Negro president of one of the colleges of the state and a Negro regional agricultural director were severely injured in an automobile collision with a white motorist just outside St. Matthews, the principal town. They were picked up by a second white motorist and brought into town. A large number of Negroes at first gathered about the car, but when they saw the bloody condition of the victims in a white man's car, none remained to offer aid, although several were intimate friends of the injured men. In the words of one person involved, "they just vanished." His explanation was that they feared there had been race trouble, and they did not want to be involved.

Although the deputy sheriff who investigated the accident said that the Negroes were clearly in the right and was willing to give this testimony in court, the lawyer who at first took their case advised them not to go to court. It was impossible, he said, for a Negro to get a verdict against a white person in that county, despite the fact of being in the right.

In 1925 a Negro farmer of the county who had amassed a fortune of some four hundred thousand dollars and who held mortgages on a leading white hotel and also on the town paving, was mysteriously shot to death from a passing automobile as he lounged about the railroad station on a Saturday evening. No one has ever been arrested for the crime, although it is commonly believed among Negroes that the killers are known. The living relative of the victim has been trying ever since to recover on notes and property, but for twenty years has been unsuccessful.

It is difficult to explain the suppressed feeling of the Negroes in the county. The county had no lynchings from 1900-1930. The condition in this county is not typical of other parts of the state. For instance, at the time of the study, a Negro was running in South Carolina for United States Senator, and was campaigning openly despite threats and warnings from whites. A reliable and observant informant attributed the suppression in Calhoun County to lack of wise and courageous leadership. For several decades, this county has had no Negro leader who would openly challenge the treatment of his people.

Most of the rural Negro ministers in this county, as in Dallas, described relations between the races as good (see Chapter Ten).

3. MISSISSIPPI COUNTY, ARKANSAS

Mississippi County in Arkansas is in the northeast corner of the state, touching the southern border of Missouri. The eastern part of the county is in the delta region, where soil is about as fertile as any on earth. Three-fourths, or 76.1 per cent, of the land of the county is devoted to cotton. About one-fifth, 20.4 per cent, is planted in corn. The soil is fabulously productive, with the result that the county is one of the world's largest cotton producing areas of its size.

Most of the land is in large plantations, which means, of course, that the county has a small number of farm owners. Thus 90.3 per cent of the farm operators are tenants. Only 14.2 per cent of the whites and 1.8 per cent of the Negro farm operators are owners. For both Negroes and whites the proportion of ownership is several times lower than in either Dallas or Calhoun Counties. One plantation was reputed to consist of 80,000 acres.

Mississippi County differs from Calhoun and Dallas in two important respects: (1) Negroes are not a majority of the population, and (2) there are more white tenants in the county than Negro.

The total population of the county in 1940 was 80,217; the Negro population was 25,069, somewhat less than one-third, 31.1 per cent. For Negroes this represented a decrease from the 1930 figure of 26,145, or 37 per cent.

Important differences were noted in economic and social conditions as compared with Calhoun and Dallas counties. One was the higher income and better living conditions of the Negro tenants. It has been found that in most communities the economic status of the white tenant, poor as it is, is still higher than that of the Negro tenant. In a county, therefore, of mixed tenancy where Negro tenants get the same wages and living conditions as white, the level of life for Negroes is somewhat higher than in sections where Negroes are the predominant tenant group. Evidences of the higher status were readily seen. Negro tenant homes were in better condition; most were painted; many were screened. It will be seen in Chapter Nine that there is greater interracial activity in this county than in Dallas or Calhoun. Arkansas is one of the states in which the Southern Tenant Farmers Union was active as an interracial organization. There is still some measure of cooperation between the two groups, although according to informants it is less than formerly obtained.

There are other phases of county life, however, that are not very much different from Calhoun or Dallas counties. Illiteracy is high, 18.6 per cent for Negroes as against 4.8 per cent for whites. However, the illiteracy rate for Negroes is not as high as it is in Dallas or Calhoun counties. The disparity in educational expenditures is large, $10.44 per Negro pupil to $23.10 per white. Yet again this difference is much smaller than that of Calhoun or Dallas, and somewhat smaller than that of Northumberland.

Racial Atmosphere

There were four lynchings in the county from 1900 to 1931, as against five in Dallas and none in Calhoun. In general, however, it appeared that the racial atmosphere here was less tense and suppressive than in Calhoun or Dallas counties. For example, a national presidential election was held at the time of the study. In the county's main town, Blytheville, many

Negroes are reported to have voted, and with the encouragement of the whites.

At the time of this study the colored population of the county was much disturbed by reports that a respectable Negro farmer had been killed by a deputy sheriff allegedly without cause. According to the reports the officer had been jailed and was awaiting trial. This is a far fairer reaction than would obtain in many Southern sections. Negro tenants openly speak of the fact that racial conditions in the county are much better than in the state of Mississippi not far away. They feel that trouble in race relations is most often caused by the Mississippi planters who settle in the county and insist on treating Negroes here as they do farther south.

Since many of the plantations are large, highly capitalized businesses, Negro tenants report that they do not have as much difficulty securing fair settlements as tenants in sections where plantations are smaller and the relations between landlord and tenant are more personal.

4. NORTHUMBERLAND COUNTY, VIRGINIA

Northumberland County is in the northeast part of Virginia, bordered on the north by the Potomac River and on the east by Chesapeake Bay.

It differs in many significant respects from the other three counties of this study. First, it is not a cotton county. The chief crops are corn and wheat. In addition the soil of the county is well adapted to truck gardening, which makes possible several cash crops as well as crops for home use. A large quantity of tomatoes are grown, and the county has a tomato canning plant.

It is not a plantation county. Only 10 per cent of the farm operators are tenants. Nearly three-fourths, 71.1 per cent, of the Negro farm operators are owners. This is in contrast to Calhoun County where the percentage of Negro ownership is 7.4, or Dallas where it is 5.4, or Mississippi, where it is 1.8.

Most significant is the varied economy of the county. Located in the Chesapeake Bay region, the county is a center of the fishing industry. Only 53.1 per cent of all Negro males are engaged in agriculture. Many work in the fish and oyster plants of the county, or on fishing vessels. A large number of those who farm also engage in fishing or oystering at various seasons of the year, to supplement their farm incomes.

The increased and steadier income makes possible a higher standard of living and the large proportion of house and farm ownership that has been noted. Negro homes seen here were by far the best of any in the four counties. In fact, this was the only county out of the four in which rural Negro homes were homes, rather than shacks or cabins. Many families keep cows, hogs, and chickens for milk and meat supply. These along with seafood and vegetable gardening make the prevailing Negro diet far better than that for any of the other counties. Incidentally, the finest example of a Negro country doctor, a physician who works tirelessly to serve the schools of the county as well as the families, was found in this county.

There is a wide disparity in educational expenditures: $130.89 per white pupil as against $68.76 per Negro. These figures were compiled for 1942. Since then a persistent effort has been made, led by a Negro minister, to secure a fairer distribution of educational funds. At the time of this study great progress had been achieved. There is now a much higher rate of pay for colored teachers in the county, approximating equality, at least on the lower levels of white salary. Also, conversations with Negro teachers and principals brought out the point that Negro education is a much more integral element in the county's educational program than it is in any of the other counties. Further, it is expected that the inadequate Negro high school building will be replaced with a modern plant in the near future. An excellent bus service for the colored high school children now operates throughout the county.

Racial Atmosphere

In the matter of racial atmosphere, there was little of the tenseness or suppression observed in other counties. In fact, race relations here were characterized by a mutually respectful cordiality that was refreshingly wholesome as compared with the "deeper" South. To be sure, the usual segregations and discriminations of Southern life obtain here, but over and above them was found a wholesome friendliness.

Church life in this county, as the succeeding chapters will show, was in many ways better than in the other three counties. There were only nine churches to cover four thousand members, an average membership of 431. Both in ministerial training and service, this county was superior to the others.

The population of the county in 1940 was 10,463, of which Negroes numbered 4,324, somewhat less than half, or 41.9 per cent.

From these brief glimpses of life in four Southern counties something may be seen of the South as a setting for the rural

Negro church. Certainly it is a setting of problems, problems that call the church forth into action, but which at the same time limit the church's ability to act. It is in this tangled area of aspirations and limitations, Christian ideals and human resistance that the rural Negro church lives and moves and seeks to clear ground for the coming of the kingdom of God.

TABLE I

CHARACTERISTICS OF THE FOUR SELECTED COUNTIES

	COUNTIES			
	Calhoun (S. C.)	Dallas (Ala.)	Mississippi (Ark.)	Northumberland (Va.)
POPULATION:				
1940	16,229	55,245	80,217	10,463
Per cent Negro	73.1	73.8	31.3	41.9
EDUCATION:				
Expenditure per white pupil	$72.82	$56.65	$23.10	$130.89
Expenditure per Negro pupil	17.54	13.45	10.44	68.76
Ratio: Negro/white expenditure	24.1	23.7	45.2	52.5
AGRICULTURE:				
Per cent of farm operators who are tenants	53.5	83.0	77.4	10.2
Per cent of white farm operators who are full owners	58.1	37.3	26.4	73.5
Per cent of Negro farm operators who are full owners	18.9	7.6	2.8	73.6
First Crop	Cotton	Cotton	Cotton	Corn
Second Crop	Corn	Corn	Corn	Wheat
LYNCHINGS: Number 1900-1945	0	5	4	1

NOTE: Whenever the words "race" and "Negro" are used it is understood that they are terms of traditional rather than scientific connotation. The large group of mixed people in America of Afro-American descent do not constitute a pure race in any sense of the word, and only a small proportion of them can be accurately termed Negro.

"Race relations" is taken to mean the behavior that white and colored people in a community manifest toward each other, particularly the effort of whites to keep Negroes in a subordinate position, and the effort of Negroes to rise out of it. The major interest here is to observe the effect of this behavior on Negro life in the areas studied and the rural church's relation to it.

Chapter Three

THE PHYSICAL CHURCH

In structure and equipment a church should serve first as a community shrine, that is, as an artistic expression of the religious mind of the community and as the seat of the community's worship. Secondly, it should serve as a center for various community activities that have as their aim the achievement of the more abundant life for all who live within reach of the church's influence. It was in the light of these two criteria that country churches were judged as to their physical adequacy to meet the basic needs of the Christian community.

For statistical sampling 130 rural churches in the four counties described in Chapter Two—Dallas, Calhoun, Mississippi, and Northumberland—were taken for detailed study. The findings of the detailed studies were checked against observations over wider areas. In general the churches were tested for (1) location, (2) construction, (3) beauty, (4) provisions for comfort, (5) facilities for outdoor activities, (6) facilities for other than regular religious activities, and (7) the state of repair of the church plant.

Location

Contrary to popular impression the majority of Negro rural churches are located on or near improved roadways, which means that they are accessible both to automobile and horse-drawn vehicles in wet and dry seasons throughout the year. Only twenty-six, or 20 per cent, of the 130 churches studied were situated back from roadways or on roads that are impassable in bad weather. More than half of the churches, 55.4 per cent, were located on or near improved roads, and 20 per cent were situated on paved main highways.

Northumberland County in Virginia had the highest percentage of churches located on paved roads, 70 per cent. All others in this county were on improved (second class) roads. It was in the plantation areas where stretches of cultivated lands are largest and the number of good roads is smallest that the rural churches suffered most from inaccessible locations.

In practically every instance the churches were located in populous communities, or in communities which until recently had been quite populous. Recent migration of families and changes in types of agriculture have left some church buildings in comparatively isolated situations, but at the time of building, the churches were placed where the people lived.

Being located in the midst of people, however, does not mean that the membership lives nearby nor that the church serves the people who are nearest. Rural families, especially landless ones, are highly mobile.[1] If a family does not move too far away, that is, if the family merely changes from one

---

[1] *Landlord and Tenant on the Cotton Plantation,* by T. J. Woofter, Chapter VI, "Mobility." Washington, D. C., Works Progress Administration, 1936.

farm to another in the same section, there is a tendency to keep membership in the old church, even though this may mean considerable travel on the "meeting" Sundays. For example, one family in Dallas County lived directly across the road from one church, but worshiped in another two and a half miles away. Also in the same county, a rural church was found that had many members who were living and working in the principal city some twelve miles distant but keeping membership in the rural church and returning regularly twice a month to services.

Construction

Of the 130 church plants visited, only four, 3.1 per cent, were constructed of brick or stone—one church in each of the four counties. The rest, 126, were wooden buildings.

Some of the wooden structures were well and solidly built, erected apparently with an eye to permanence, comfort and utility. Many more, however, were poorly, cheaply, and even roughly built, constructed apparently in response to a hasty and poorly considered desire to have a meeting hall for occasional religious gatherings, rather than to have a permanent, inspiring community shrine.

Of the 130 churches studied, only 26.2 per cent were rated as first class. For the four counties the first class ratings were: Calhoun county, 31.2 per cent; Dallas county, 18.3 per cent; Mississippi county, 10.7 per cent. In Northumberland county alone the churches were uniformly of excellent construction. Here they were built on strong foundations, of good materials, and sealed inside with wood or plaster. In the other three counties the churches rated as poor, constituting 24.6

per cent of the total, were built of cheap or rough materials, were often unsealed inside, and frequently were drafty from cracks in the weatherboarding. Approximately one-half of all the churches visited, 49.2 per cent, were rated as medium, which indicated that some of the construction features were unsatisfactory.

This cheapness of construction is one of the factors responsible for the disparity in the value of rural and urban churches. According to the United States Census of Religious Bodies, 1936, the average urban Negro church is valued at $10,126. The value of the average rural Negro church is less than one-fifth as much, $1,990.[1]

In considering the condition and value of rural churches, one or two qualifying facts must be kept in mind. Shabby construction is obviously the result of many causes, chief of which are the poverty of the people, their educational and cultural limitations, and the lack of best religious leadership. Seventy-three per cent of all Negro farmers are tenants or wage hands possessing little land and little community security.[2] When the meagerness of their annual income is taken into account along with the other handicaps of tenant status, it is surprising that only 24.6 per cent of the churches studied are of the "poor" type. In other words, the rural churches, poor as they are, represent a major effort on the part of a handicapped people to express their love of God and their desire to worship him.

[1] *Religious Bodies*: 1936, Vol. I, p. 855. Washington, D. C., United States Department of Commerce, Bureau of the Census.
[2] *Sixteenth Census of the United States*, 1940, Agriculture, Vol. III, pp. 139, 164, 165.

Beauty

Many of the 130 churches were located on sites of great natural beauty. In cases where the sites were not beautiful, they could with very little effort be made so. Located in the South where the climate is temperate, rainfall abundant, and vegetation in most cases luxuriant, beauty of setting is not only easily attainable, it is almost inescapable.

Yet out of 130 churches, only twelve, or 9.2 per cent, had any kind of cultivated flowers around them, and only twenty-four, 18.4 per cent, had shrubbery of any kind.

In spite of obvious indifference and neglect, nature had contrived to surround many of the churches with trees and vegetation that gave them an almost jewel-like setting. For example, in Dallas County, one moderate-sized church sat in the midst of a large cotton plantation. There was nothing to break the montony of the flat, cultivated view save this rural church surrounded by a few trees. To come upon this scene at cotton picking time when the fields were white and nothing but white, except in the center a cluster of green-gold trees protecting a little gleaming white church nestled in their midst—here was a scene of breath-taking beauty. Yet save for the paint on the church, all of this beauty was unplanned and probably unintended.

Ninety-two, or 71 per cent, of the churches were painted. Most of them were painted white, many had been painted recently. It appeared that the rural church is awakening to an appreciation of the place of beauty in religious living.

Eleven of the churches had stained glass or frosted glass windows, 83 had painted windows, 28 had plain windows with wooden shutters, and 8 had wooden shutters with no glass panes.

Comfort

Provisions for comfort are just as necessary to the rural worshiper as to the urban. In fact, the rural worshiper probably needs them more since he often travels miles to his church and is away from home for longer periods. The country Christian often spends the whole of Sunday at his church, staying through the morning, afternoon, and evening activities. Distance and difficulty of travel make this necessary. Facilities for rest, for refreshment, and for other needs are imperative. Yet it is in the matter of providing for the comfort of its members that the rural church seems to have been least thoughtful.

Only eighteen of the 130 churches had outdoor benches for the use of those attending services. Anyone who has spent a day at a rural church knows the awkwardness of the interim hours between services or "meetings." As a rule there is nowhere to sit save inside the church, which in summer is hot and in winter is cold. Most of those who remain outside sit on the runningboards of automobiles, if an unoccupied runningboard or fender can be found. It is not uncommon for a visitor with an automobile to come out of a service and find every seat in his car filled with uninvited occupants he probably has never seen before. Only three churches in Calhoun, five in Dallas, four in Mississippi, and six in Northumberland counties had any outdoor benches at all, and in no case was the number of benches adequate. The lack of facilities for rest and relaxation is hardest on the young, who often must wait long hours between activities intended for them.

The same can be said of play facilities for the smaller children. Only three out of 130 churches, 2.3 per cent, had made any provision for children's play. Yet rural children stay at church for long periods waiting for their parents. Simple, inexpensive play facilities such as swings, see-saws, or slides, can easily be had in any rural community. However, only one church in Mississippi County, one in Dallas, and one in Northumberland had anything at all with which their children could play.

One is at a loss to explain this lack of simple, necessary conveniences. Possibly it is due to the lack of thoughtfulness on the part of laymen and leaders, or it may reflect the traditional disfavor with which recreation in any form is still viewed in some Southern communities. Three ministers stated that it is impossible to keep benches and facilities around a church that is used only once or twice a month. If the fixtures are not carried away, they are soon ruined by exposure to weather. This does not explain, however, why lockers or sheds could not be provided for storing the facilities when they are not in use.

Seventy-two churches had their own sources of water, in two cases a spring near by, in other cases a well or a pump. When the church stood near a school, the tendency was for the church to use the school's water as well as other facilities. Fifty-eight churches had no water supply at all. In such cases a bucket of water was borrowed from a farmhouse if one was near, and if not, there would be no water available during services, unless members brought their own. One informant told how when his church wanted to raise money for digging a well at the church, he opposed it, saying, "To my recollection, no one in this church has perished for lack of water in forty years." He did not see why a well was needed now.

In several cases the single bucket and dipper was found to be still in use. The tendency for all to drink from the same dipper is decreasing, however, especially among the younger folk. This appears to be a positive result of the persistent teaching of rural health workers.

Since the rural worshiper spends most of the day at his church, provision of adequate, sanitary toilet facilities is imperative. Yet only 46.9 per cent of the churches had two toilets —one for males and one for females; 29.9 per cent had only one toilet for both sexes, and 22.6 per cent had no toilets at all. Even where toilets were provided, they often were in disrepair, unsightly and unsanitary. Some were located in grassy or weedy spots that discouraged their use for fear of snakes.

The matter of adequate toilets assumes an increased importance when it is remembered that these facilities are used by growing boys and girls and become part of their training in decency, to say nothing of personal cleanliness. Indeed, it appears that the state of toilet facilities is an insight into a congregation's appreciation of some of the nicer elements of wholesome living.

As in the case of water supply, when a church was located near a school, the church generally made use of the school's toilet facilities.

Forty-nine churches, 36.9 per cent, had electric lights. In all others the lighting was by kerosene lamps, with the exception of two cases in which gasoline mantle lamps were used. In many cases where electric lights were not used it was because no power lines ran through the vicinity. In most cases where churches had electricity, the lights were open bulbs suspended from ceilings in improper and annoying positions.

Needless to say, the light from kerosene lamps suspended from ceilings or hung at intervals on side walls is inadequate. Reading by such lamps is difficult, if not impossible. Also, when a lighted lamp is set upon a lectern which an animated preacher vigorously pounds, kerosene lighting is dangerous.

Facilities for Outdoor Meetings

In the South summers are long and seasons are mild. Many activities of the rural church are held out of doors a large part of the year. Meals served at conferences or conventions, the selling of refreshments, small gatherings such as study groups or Sunday school classes, are held on the grounds around the church. Permanent provision for these activities would seem to be in order, such as tables, benches, shelters, pavillions, or even cleared spaces in shaded spots. However, only eight churches out of the one hundred and thirty had made provision of any kind. Four had booths or sheds for selling refreshments, eight had tables made of long planks laid atop stakes driven into the ground. Two churches had wiring for outdoor electric lights.

Extra Rooms

Most striking in the study of rural church plants was the scarcity of rooms, such as choir rooms, pastor's studies, Sunday school rooms, rest rooms, or rooms for the preparing and serving of food. The great majority of the churches were built to the simple floor plan of a door at one end and a rostrum at the other, with only benches for the worshipers in between. It should be said again, however, that rooms for comfort, retirement and smaller gatherings are just as necessary or more so, to the country churchman as to the urban.

Only in Northumberland County did all of the churches in a county have at least two smaller rooms, one of which could be used as a pastor's study. Of 130 churches in the four counties, 37 had choir rooms and 32 had rooms used as pastor's studies. Only five out of the total had rooms of any kind other than these. The conclusion seems inescapable that such simple provisions have not yet come to be regarded as essential elements in the life and thinking of a rural people trained to crude, limited living. Also, a pastor's study is hardly necessary to a pastor whose time in his parish is generally one or two days a month, or less.

Present Conditions

Of the 130 churches studied, only 52, or 40 per cent, were reported in good repair. The remainder in various ways were in need of repairing. Twenty-seven churches were undergoing repairs at the time the study was made. Several ministers stated that repairs or rebuilding would be undertaken as soon as materials and labor could be secured.

A number of other factors were considered in this study. One of these was heating. Very few of the churches were adequately heated. One church was heated by steam and three by hot air furnaces located in the basements of the churches. All others were heated by furnaces or stoves placed in the open body of the church. In the poorer churches, which were cracked and drafty, sitting through a service with heat that was not uniform and often insufficient was a hardship. Yet few words of complaint were heard from members who attended Sunday after Sunday under such conditions.

In the matter of pews or seats it was observed that in a few churches, mostly in Northumberland county, finished comfortable pews were used. In all other cases the seats were benches made of wooden strips, which generally were quite comfortable.

In pulpit arrangement a common pattern was followed in most cases: at the back end of the church a square rostrum with a lectern in the center, three or four chairs on the rostrum behind the lectern for ministers and guests, and behind the seats or on either side of the rostrum chairs for a choir. Some of the larger churches, especially those close to small towns, had more elaborate arrangements. One of the most beautiful pulpit arrangements seen was that of a newly built rural church in Northumberland County that had a large, illuminated picture of the Shepherd Christ directly behind and slightly above the pulpit. It afforded a most impressive setting for a rural church service.

In some cases the interiors of the churches were painted in restful, attractive colors that were quite conducive to worship. In many other cases, however, the interior colors were badly chosen, clearly the work of inexperienced hands. With the poorer churches, most interiors were not painted at all.

Cemeteries were adjacent to forty-six of the churches studied. In a few instances these were well kept. In two cases they were fenced. In most cases they were unkempt and badly overgrown with grasses and weeds, making location of graves difficult, to say the least.

While the study did not include parsonages, it was found that only 13 churches out of the 130 had parsonages located near the churches. Ninety per cent of the ministers lived away from their charges.[1] This was true even where the minister farmed in the church community. Generally he lived in his own home, and transacted most of the church's business from there.

Notable Instances

The figures presented in this chapter give a general idea of prevailing conditions. They cannot describe the many exceptional individual cases that were found. It has already been mentioned that one of the finest churches seen, both in beauty and utility, was in the middle of a cotton plantation in Dallas County. One of the most commodious rural churches was a recently built brick church in Northumberland County that had a concrete basement used for Sunday school and small meetings, a steam heating plant, a large, comfortable auditorium, and grounds that the congregation planned to landscape and equip for outdoor activities. But again, these are striking exceptions. They serve, however, as expressions of possibilities.

In one of the rudest of all the churches seen—unpainted, unsealed, its steps falling down, large cracks in the floor, the seats broken or patched with rough wood—in this church someone with a sense of beauty had placed two large jars of beautiful artificial flowers at each end of the uncertain

[1] See Chapter Six.

rostrum, and had hung pretty flowered curtains at windows that frequently lacked panes.

Summary

This study of the physical condition of rural churches in four Southern counties has shown that while a few rural churches meet the needs of the rural Christian in most ways, many of the churches do not. Few churches have made adequate provision for the comfort or convenience of their members. Few are adequate aesthetic expressions of the regard that the people have for their God and for his house.

Out of 130 churches, only 34, or 26.2 per cent, could be rated as first class; 64, or 49.2 per cent, were rated as medium, and 32, or 24.6 per cent, were rated as poor.

In seeking causes for the physical inadequacy of the rural church, we can find them easily. The poverty of the people, their educational and cultural limitations, and above all the lack of enlightened, well trained leadership are factors apparently most responsible for present conditions.

It appears that the major responsibility for conditions must be laid at the door of ministerial leadership. To be sure, a poorly built and poorly kept church edifice is a sign of the religious level of the worshiping group. Yet many rural churches even in these difficult times are undergoing extensive repairs, and as the study will show later, rural congregations are giving generously of their limited means for the maintenance and improvement of their churches.[1] This would seem to indicate that where effective leadership is at hand, worthy results may be achieved.

[1] Chapter Five.

It was generally found that wherever a beautiful, adequate church had been built in a rural community, the people spoke with highest appreciation of the leader who had guided them through the achievement.

The prevalence of repairing and efforts to beautify, even if no more than painting the church, seem to indicate an increasing awareness of the need for beauty in the religious life of the country Christian.

Chapter Four

MEMBERSHIP

The impression appears to be widespread that country people are generally religious and that most if not all of them are church members. This is regarded as especially true of Negroes. The impression, however, is not true to the facts. Among Negroes, as among whites, rural church membership varies widely. In some sections it is high, in others it is low. It is directly affected by the economic and social levels upon which the people live.

For example, in Northumberland County, Virginia, a county in which farm ownership, family income, and the general cultural level is high, church membership among the people of the county is high, 89.7 per cent. On the other hand, in Mississippi County, Arkansas, a predominantly tenant area in which farm ownership, family income, and general cultural level are all low, church membership is also low, only 10 per cent.

These figures for Negroes in rural sections closely parallel the same percentages for whites. It is now known that tenants and other disadvantaged agricultural people are not overly given to church membership. Their mobility, their poverty, their lack of "belonging" to their communities, their lack of educational development, all tend to reduce not only church membership among them, but also the quality of church life and leadership offered to them. This fact deserves the serious attention of church bodies in considering the service of the church in needy areas.[1]

In the county studies it was found that the churches varied considerably in size from county to county. The largest churches were in Northumberland County, which had only nine churches to 3,880 members, an average of 431 members per church. A very large church of 900 members was found in this county. The smallest churches were in Mississippi County, in which twenty-two churches out of twenty-five had 1,790 members, an average membership of 81. This county had the smallest single church, one with a membership of only ten. The national average membership for Negro rural churches is 109.[2] Thus, Northumberland County is nearly four times the average, 431; Calhoun is considerably above it, 188; on the basis of fifty-two churches studied, Dallas County is a little below, 107; and Mississippi County, with 81, is much below the national Negro rural average.

One interesting phase of rural church membership was the proportion of young people, which tended to remain fairly constant despite the variations in membership-to-population

[1] Table II indicates the proportion of church members in the populations of three counties.

[2] *Religious Bodies*: 1936, Vol. I, p. 856. Washington, D. C., United States Department of Commerce, Bureau of the Census.

TABLE II
PERCENTAGE OF NEGRO POPULATION WHO ARE
CHURCH MEMBERS IN THREE COUNTIES

COUNTY	NEGRO POPULATION	CHURCH MEMBERSHIP	PERCENTAGE IN COUNTY
Northumberland	4,324	3,880	89.7
Calhoun	11,869	5,821	49.0
Mississippi	25,069	2,500[1]	10.0

[1] The estimated total attendance of twenty-five churches.

ratios. In Calhoun County the young people, that is, persons under twenty years of age, numbered 1,301 or 22.4 per cent of the total church membership; in Dallas County they numbered 1,561 or 26.2 per cent; in Mississippi County, 419 or 24.0 per cent; and in Northumberland County, 1,040 or 26.8 per cent. While the percentage is highest in Northumberland County and lowest in Calhoun, it tends to approximate one-fourth in each of the counties, as it does in the total, 25.3 per cent.

Membership Gains

Most churches reported gains in membership during the year preceding this study. Although these gains were not sufficient to offset losses that in many cases were serious, there were only a few churches that did not take in some new persons in the course of the year. Three churches in Calhoun County, ten in Dallas, four in Mississippi and one in Northumberland reported no increase in membership. In several cases in which no gain was reported the lack of increase was due to the fact that there were no unchurched persons in the community.

A large number of new members did not necessarily indicate an active church, nor a small number an inactive one. In many rural communities, especially the smaller ones, there may be few persons who are not church members. In such a case a small increase would point to an active church that had already done its work of evangelizing. One such instance was found in Northumberland County. A revival was held in one of the churches for five successive nights without a single convert. The pastor knew at the time that there was but one "sinner" in the community, an old man. The pastor said he did not expect the old man to repent, for he was "certain that the Devil already has him."

TABLE III

MEMBERSHIP INCREASE IN FOUR COUNTIES IN THE YEAR 1944

COUNTY	NUMBER OF MEMBERS	INCREASE IN MEMBERS	PER CENT INCREASE
Calhoun (31 churches)	5,821	536	9.2
Dallas (52 churches)	5,571	351	6.3
Mississippi (22 churches)	1,790	261	14.6
Northumberland (9 churches)	3,880	140	3.6
All Counties	17,062	1,288	7.5

Methods of Seeking New Members

In all but two instances, the only methods used by 114 churches to win new members were the revival and the invitation extended at regular services. In two cases the pastors reported that they used personal or visitation evangelism as a planned method of seeking new members. No others used the method and few seemed to know about it.

Exclusive use of the older methods is due to (1) survival of old custom, (2) the absentee pastorate, and (3) lack of acquaintance with new methods.

The old-fashioned revival, held generally in the summer or early fall, is one of the most fixed of rural practices. The weaknesses of the method, such as the instability of revival converts, and the unwholesome social practices that often accompany revival meetings, have little effect on the revival's popularity. It is still the chief means of winning converts to Christianity in rural sections.

In addition to special or seasonal evangelistic efforts, there is at every preaching service a period when the "doors of the church are opened" and persons are invited to join. The invitation usually follows the sermon. Despite the revival's popularity, most members are taken into the church in this way. These two means are customs, but they are also practically the only methods that can be used by pastors who do not live among their people, and therefore have little contact with the people of the community outside their own memberships.

Three pastors reported that they had an annual Decision Day when young people of the Sunday school were urged to join the church. This is a comparatively recent innovation in the country that is confined to the larger churches. It does not eliminate the revival, since it is intended mainly for the young.

One progressive young pastor sought to institute a Week of Prayer as a substitute for the revival. He hoped this would provide an escape from the revival's undesirable features and unwholesome effects. Also, since there were few unchurched persons in his community, the revival as a means of seeking converts was unnecessary. After two years, at the time of this study, the Week of Prayer was still observed the first week in each year, but also in the fall the old type of preaching revival was held as a concession to the older persons who were very much dissatisfied with its omission. He stated that he had to restore it for the sake of peace.

Membership Losses: Migration

The gains in membership reported above seldom were net gains. Indeed, in sharp contrast to the increases reported were the cases of losses in membership, many of them so great as to reduce materially the size of some churches, and in a few cases, to close the churches completely. All the cases of extreme loss were due to migration or emigration of the members from rural to urban centers, and according to many reports, from Southern to Northern or Western regions.

As has been previously mentioned, this study was made in wartime, a period when the movement of people from country to city, from section to section, was greatly accelerated. Further, many men and some women were temporarily drawn away from the rural sections for service in the armed forces, or for labor in war industries.

Apart from war conditions, agricultural methods in the South were undergoing radical changes. Increasing mechanization and large scale farming, the change from cotton growing to cattle raising, all were reducing the number of field hands needed in the rural South.

In the midst of a vast shifting in a large part of the population, it was difficult to get accurate contemporary figures, or to determine causes and effects. Some questions that naturally arose could hardly be well answered at the moment. For example, was the migration a permanent movement, or was it a temporary change in place of living in response to wartime demands? Would there be a return of both soldiers and civilians to the soil after the war? Would the poorer Southern farmers remaining on the soil, who for the most part were landless farmers, be able to compete with the large, highly capitalized farms, which were increasingly setting up in Southern regions? All of these questions have a profound bearing upon Southern rural community life and the Southern rural church. They are crucial considerations from the viewpoint of the rural church's future.

A number of exhaustive studies of Negro migration have been made in recent years. One by Louise Venable Kennedy, published in 1929, covers the period prior to the first world war and the decade following.[1] A second study by Richard Sterner and others, under the sponsorship of the Carnegie Corporation, investigates the whole question carefully and in addition covers the period from 1930 to 1940.[2] A third by Lyonel C. Florant[3] is an unpublished manuscript that forms the basis for the chapter on migration in *An American Dilemma*.

All three of these studies reveal that the heavy movement of Negroes from rural to urban sections is not of recent origin. Always highly mobile, even from point to point within the

[1] *The Negro Peasant Turns Cityward,* by Louise Venable Kennedy. New York, Columbia University Press, 1930.

[2] *The Negro's Share,* by Richard Sterner. New York, Harper and Brothers, 1943.

[3] *Negro Migration* 1860-1940, by Lyonel C. Florant. Unpublished manuscript prepared for the Carnegie Study, 1940; revised edition 1942. Harlem Branch of the New York Public Library.

South itself, since 1910 the Negro has moved with such rapidity that Sterner calls it a "flight from agriculture."

According to Kennedy, in the ten years from 1910 to 1920, the Negro population of New York State increased 47.9 per cent, that of Illinois 67.1 per cent, and that of Michigan 251.0 per cent. During this period the increase in Negro population for the whole nation was only 6.5 per cent. To show further the movement from South to North, in the same period that the Negro population of the North was phenomenally increasing, the Negro population of the state of Mississippi decreased 7.4 per cent.[1]

It was about 1910 that Negroes from the "deep" Southern states began to move North in appreciable numbers. Prior to that time the majority of Negroes came from the more northern states of the South, such as Virginia and Kentucky. In 1920, however, it was found that the percentage of Negroes from the cotton belt states had increased from 18.2 per cent to 40.5 per cent in the preceding decade.[2]

Sterner shows that the movement northward continued through the 1930's, in spite of the depression and its unemployment of those years. He also shows that Negroes are leaving Southern agriculture much more rapidly than whites.

By comparing figures from the census reports of 1920, 1930, and 1940, we see that the Negro rural farm population of the South decreased 8.6 per cent between 1920 and 1930, whereas the decrease in white farm population for the same period was 3.0 per cent. In 1930 to 1940 the percentage of Negro decrease

[1] Kennedy, *op. cit.*, pp. 26 ff. Used by permission.
[2] "Recent Northward Migration of the Negro," by Joseph A. Hill in *Monthly Labor Review,* Vol. XVIII, March, 1924, pp. 475-88.

was 4.5, while there was a small increase for whites. In other words, in the third decade the exodus of Negroes from the farm was only about half as heavy as in the preceding decade, but it was still much greater than that for whites.

TABLE IV

PER CENT INCREASE OR DECREASE (−) IN RURAL-FARM POPULATION[1]

1930–1940		1920–1930	
COLORED	WHITE	COLORED	WHITE
−4.5	2.1	−8.6	−3.0

[1] Sterner, *op. cit.*, pp. 11 ff.   Used by permission.

Something of the rural population loss in the four counties of this study may be seen in Table V. From April 1, 1940, to November 1, 1943, Northumberland County lost 1,891 people, or 18.1 per cent of its population; Calhoun County lost 2,777, or 17.1 per cent; Dallas lost 4,349, or 7.9 per cent, and Mississippi County lost 2,659, or 3.3 per cent. These figures are totals, and are not divided on the basis of color. They were derived from ration book registrations, and hence the decrease would include persons who went into the armed services as well as civilians who moved from rural to urban points. It seems fair to assume, however, that a large proportion of the loss was Negro, and that it will be permanent. There are several grounds for this assumption.

First, if population trends during the present post-war period are to be similar to those after the last war, many of those who have left will not return to the farms. It has just been seen that in two decades from 1920 to 1940, Negro rural population continued to decline, even during the depression.

TABLE V
ESTIMATED CHANGE IN POPULATION[1] OF FOUR COUNTIES

COUNTY	POPULATION		ESTIMATED CHANGE APRIL 1, 1940 TO Nov. 1, 1943	
	Nov. 1943	April 1940	Number	Per Cent
Calhoun	13,452	16,229	−2,777	−17.1
Dallas	50,896	55,245	−4,349	− 7.9
Mississippi	77,558	80,217	−2,659	− 3.3
Northumberland	8,572	10,463	−1,891	−18.1

[1] "Estimated Civilian Population of the United States, by Counties: November 1, 1943," *Special Reports*, Series P-44, No. 3. Washington, D. C., United States Department of Commerce, Bureau of the Census, 1944.

This indicates that there was not a sufficient return even to balance the heavy migration of 1910 to 1920.

Second, since Negroes are not taken into Southern industry in the same proportion as are whites, it is more necessary for them to leave the county, even the South, in order to obtain work in industry.

A number of factors are suggested as being causes of the heavy Negro migration: the hardships and insecurity of tenant life; the discriminations and indignities visited upon Negroes in the South; the hope of better wages; better life in northern cities; the boll weevil; soil erosion; the "one-or-two-crop gamble"; the movement of cotton production to the Southwest and West; the general over-production of cotton; the AAA reductions in cash crop acreage; increasing mechanization; and the increase in cattle raising.[1] Kennedy adds the influence of relatives and friends who have settled in other sections, as being a strong force leading to migration.[2] One in-

[1] Sterner, *op. cit.*, p. 12.
[2] Kennedy, *op. cit.*, Chapter II, "The Causes of Migration."

clusive paragraph seems to express the entire question well:

Fundamentally, behind Negro movements, as behind those of any people, there must be a dissatisfaction with conditions in the present location and the promise of improvement in some other region. . . . The causes of migration may be grouped under those which are "driving" and those which are "beckoning." . . . In the case of recent Negro migrations the "push" which has been of dominant influence has been the inability to make a satisfactory living in the black belt, while the principal "pull" has been the prospect of greater economic opportunities in northern industries. In spite of the general predominance of this economic motive, the influence of social conditions should not be overlooked, for the discriminations and disadvantages which have burdened the southern Negroes have resulted in a feeling of discontent and restlessness which, in turn, have tended to a ready belief in promises of better conditions. Once started, the migration has been strengthened by discussions, letters, newspaper propaganda, the desire to join relatives and friends and, at first, the suggestion resulting from a mass movement.[1]

The matter of migration has been considered in some detail, for it is not only determinative of rural church membership, but it is the one force that can eliminate the rural church itself.

From the point of view of this study, the discussion raises three questions vital to the welfare of the rural church. First, what effect has migration had on the rural church so far? Second, what is the probable future of migration? How long will the great exodus continue, and how many Negroes will move? Third, what is the attitude of rural ministers toward the migration of their members, and what should they do, what *can* they do about it?

[1] Kennedy, *op. cit.*, p. 41.

In answer to the first question it has to be said at once that no reliable figures are available for measuring the growth or decline of the Negro rural church. This applies even to the United States census of religious bodies.

Separate figures for rural and urban churches were not compiled until the religious bodies census of 1926. The census for that year shows 32,427 Negro rural churches with a membership of 2,964,616. The census of ten years later, 1936, shows 24,775 churches with a membership of 2,701,988—an apparent loss of 7,652 churches and 262,628 members. It is found upon closer study, however, that this loss is apparent, rather than actual. It is due, as the census itself states, to the faulty returns made by many Negro churches.[1] An extreme case in point is that of the African Methodist Episcopal Church. According to the census, this denomination had in 1926 in the State of Texas 640 churches with a membership of 33,985. The census for 1936 shows 21 churches with a membership of 1,170, a decrease of 619 churches and 32,815 members, which if real would mean the virtual elimination of this church in Texas.

Yet according to officials of this denomination, no such loss has taken place. Texas still is one of the leading states in the African Methodist Church. The trouble is that the Texas churches of this denomination failed to report in 1936.

The census of religious bodies makes its enumerations chiefly through questionnaires. A high proportion of faulty returns, especially from rural areas, is almost to be expected. This means, unfortunately, that at the present time we simply do not have trustworthy figures for judging the growth or decline of the Negro rural church.

[1] *Religious Bodies*: 1936, Vol. I, p. 85.

Since there is a steady loss in rural Negro population due chiefly to migration, it is fair to assume that there is a corresponding loss in church membership. But it certainly is not as great as the 8.8 per cent loss indicated in the census for 1936.

Any answer to the second question—that is, how long will the exodus continue, and how many Negroes will move—is of course a matter of opinion. A number of persons in responsible positions were queried on the subject. While opinions varied, a few general conclusions were obtained:

1. The heavy migration of Negroes from the South to other sections of the country will continue for one or two decades at least. The causes of migration, already mentioned, are still operative. It will take years to correct some of them.

2. Not all Negroes will wish to leave the rural South. There are cases of highly successful Negro farmers. There are also cases of Negroes who enjoy respect and comparative security in their communities. At the present time they are the rare exceptions, but they stand as possibilities. Other Negroes of industry and ability may also be able to achieve similar advantages.

3. It is possible that the decrease in the number of Negroes in the South will lessen fears, antipathies, and tensions.

4. As the "Promised Land" view of the North and West tends to die away, and the hardships of city life become known, and above all, as Negroes generally come to recognize that life either North or South is filled with responsibilities, there will be less tendency to move carelessly from place to place.

5. At the present time, there is a tendency among Negroes to regard agriculture as an undesirable, if not shameful, vocation. The reason for such a feeling is that most Negroes have

engaged in agriculture only on the very lowest levels. In addition, the Negro has shared the feeling, which is still widespread in America, that urban life is better than rural. If agriculture can be shown to be a worthy vocation for Negroes as well as whites, there will be less tendency to flee it. A number of educational and social agencies, such as vocational schools, and Federal and state extension services, are seeking to create in the rural Negro a feeling of respect for agriculture as a way of life.

6. Since the beginning of this century, numerous Federal and state agencies have been established to help the landless, disadvantaged classes in American agriculture. Negroes have shared and will share in whatever advances are achieved. As life on the Southern farm becomes more "livable," Negroes will be less impelled to leave.

7. More than half the persons interviewed were hopeful of improvements in the social, economic, and political conditions now confronting Southern Negroes. As more of the benefits sought by migration become established in the South, there will be less need for migration.

8. More than half of the leaders felt that progress is slowly but steadily being achieved in the South. They point to progress in education, in politics, in fuller interracial cooperation. Hope is seen in the Supreme Court decision requiring Southern states to provide equal higher education and in the same court's ruling that railroads must provide equal accommodations for all passengers in interstate traffic. They see further hope in the fact that some labor unions in the South are trying to eliminate discriminatory practices among their white and colored members. The respondents felt that as whites grow in

fair-mindedness, and Negroes in ability to bear a full share of social and economic responsibility, progress will come.

9. All the persons queried felt that some of the present migration is necessary and good. It will draw off displaced farm labor and will give some of the poverty-stricken masses in Southern agriculture a chance at a better life. Those who remain may have an opportunity to achieve a higher standard of living.

This last point is supported by a case found in Dallas County, Alabama. Most of the colored citizens of a community had left it. The whites who owned the farm land lived in the city fifteen miles away and rented the land to Negroes or used colored sharecroppers. The scarcity of labor resulting from the migration had made farming so difficult that most white landlords were willing to sell their holdings and give up farming. The Negroes who remained used funds that had accumulated in two burial societies to buy large tracts of land at low rates, which they then resold to colored buyers in smaller plots at low interest rates for the establishment of homesteads. The effort is favored with excellent leaders, particularly one man whose work has been outstanding. If the venture is successful, a little community of self-sustaining people will one day be found where tenants and farmhands formerly lived.

The third question remains: What is the attitude of the rural minister toward the migration of his members, and what does he plan to do about it? Sixty-two ministers were asked their views of the matter. The attitudes were of three distinct types, approving, indifferent, disapproving.

1. Twenty-nine, or 46.8 per cent of the ministers, definitely favored migration. Most regarded it as a welcome escape for

their people from unfortunate conditions. Although their ministries had done little to alleviate conditions, the ministers were keenly aware of the wrongs under which their people suffered, and were glad to see them relieved. In cases where the leaving of large numbers worked a hardship on landlords, they regarded this as an overdue "getting even."

2. Twenty-six ministers, 41.9 per cent, were indifferent; that is, their feelings on the question were not strong enough to result in a decided opinion. They felt the people should go if they wanted, or be able to stay if they pleased. As to any upsets that migration might cause in their ministerial careers, they likewise were indifferent. They felt they could preach wherever the people happened to be, in country or in town. Several of these ministers had held pastorates in Northern cities, and a large proportion of them go North frequently, if not annually, to conduct revivals or special meetings in churches in Northern cities made up largely of Southern people. Since their chief concern is preaching, the place where they preach is of little moment.

3. A small group, twelve, or 19.4 per cent, disapproved of the leaving of their people. Some of the reasons were sentimental. The departure of a large part of a community greatly changes its life and form. These ministers hated to see the old ways changed, and those they loved going away.

Some of the reasons were more practical. Not all of the families that migrate prosper. Some run into misfortune. This was true of great numbers during the depression years. Many rural communities have persons, sometimes families, that tried to live in the new Northern environment, but, not being able to stay there, had to return South. To many, these returned migrants are like birds with broken wings, and they stand as reminders that all is not perfect bliss in the North. Not a few of the ministers resented the fact that their people had to flee from the land which they had long tended, and which should be their heritage. Nearly all of the ministers who opposed migration felt that Negroes should not run from the difficulties of Southern agriculture, but should stay and work them out. They held to the hope that conditions could be improved, and that a way somehow would be found out of the troubles.

Of the sixty-two ministers, about 80 per cent were not seriously disturbed about the effect of migration upon the rural church. Twelve ministers were concerned, but as far as could be learned were doing nothing to counteract it. To be sure, the only offset to migration is wholesome community life that makes migration unnecessary. Yet as will be shown later, in the matter of making better communities few rural pastors have anything to offer.

One reason for lack of concern over the effects of migration is that there is a serious shortage of ministers in rural areas. Almost any pastor today can find a church of some kind. This is partly accountable for the fact that some ministers have three, four, and in a few cases even more churches. If a church is too greatly hampered by loss of members, the pastor can usually find another church without great difficulty.

In spite of the heavy loss in membership through migration, only three churches were found that had been closed. The general tendency is for the members remaining to carry on the church program, even though the number may not be sufficient to justify it, and the financial burden of maintaining the church falls very heavily on the few.

A striking case in point is that of a church in Calhoun County located in a community that has been greatly stripped of its population. The town has the appearance of a deserted village. The church in question fifteen years ago had a membership of two hundred fifty, and was one of the outstanding churches in the vicinity. Today the membership is twelve, all middle-aged or old people. The church building is in decay, a large part of the roof is falling in, and the floor is being warped by rain. Plaster falls from the walls, and the large church bell that formerly called the community to worship had to be taken from the roofless steeple for fear it would fall through the floor of the church. The parsonage, which once was a respectable residence for a pastor, is now closed and boarded, uninhabited for years. Yet in this atmosphere of rot and desertion, the twelve members meet regularly once a month for service. They meet in the church when the weather is good, and in a home when it is not. An aged pastor serves them, and funds are raised to meet the church expenses. Whatever else may be said of this, it is an expression of firm loyalty to a cause.

Out of fifty churches in Dallas County, thirty, 59.9 per cent, reported a loss in membership from migration of members. Of twenty-two churches in Mississippi County, eighteen, 81.8 per cent, reported loss, and in Calhoun County, twenty-two out of thirty-two, or 68.7 per cent.

Because of inaccurate record keeping (see below) it was not possible to get the extent of loss exactly. Some idea can be gained, however, from individual cases. A church in Mississippi County that five years ago had 400 members, now has 200; another that three years ago had 260 members, today has

55. A most extreme case is a church in Dallas County that six years ago had 700 members, and now has but 115.

Record Keeping

In all cases except two, membership records were kept in a roll book by a church secretary or church clerk. In two cases an index card system was used. Invariably the clerk or secretary kept the record at his home. In no case was the record kept at a church office and in only one case did a pastor possess a duplicate membership record. In many cases the pastor did not regard keeping the membership record as his responsibility. This was especially true among the non-resident pastors.

In a few cases the church clerks were educated, qualified persons who kept accurate records of the membership, as well as of the activities of the church. In one county two exceptional instances were found in which exact current records were maintained, and have been maintained through the years. From these records splendid church histories have been compiled.

In the majority of cases, however, the church clerks were worthy, well meaning persons but were unqualified for the task of keeping records. They were poorly educated, and in some cases able to write only with difficulty. Although thus limited, they frequently were the best the congregation afforded. It is only natural that such persons would not appreciate the value of records, and that such as were kept would be most unsatisfactory.

The record books of sixty churches were examined in some detail. In most cases, names of persons long dead were still found listed as living members. Names of persons who long had moved away and had since maintained no contact with the church, were still carried as members. In several cases the names of persons claiming membership in churches were not to be found in the roll books.

The membership records were checked periodically, varying from once a month to once a year. The general practice appeared to be once a quarter. In general, payment of dues was the criterion of church membership. Few cases of withdrawal or dismissal for any other reason were found.

Such loose record keeping means that the rural church can have little formal follow-up of its members. When members leave the community, little is known of what happens after that, or of their further religious life. Occasionally a letter of dismission or transfer is sent when a former member wishes to join a church elsewhere.

In contrast to the other counties, the churches of Northumberland County have a means of keeping contact with their members that seems to be most effective. It is done through alumni clubs. When members leave the community to work or live in other places, careful records are kept. If a number of members live in the same town, an alumni club is formed, much on the order of a college alumni club. Once or twice a year the pastor visits the clubs and preaches to them in a special service. In addition, he counsels them in any needed way. One pastor reported that during the past year alone he had induced five of his members working in a Northern defense center to invest a good share of their large wartime earnings in farm land in the home community.

The churches of Northumberland County also observe an annual Home-Coming Day. Once a year, usually in the fall, all members who are away are invited to return to the home church. With most of the churches this is a gala occasion. Members travel great distances to attend.

In these two ways the Northumberland rural churches maintain an intimate and constant contact with their members that is most unusual for country churches.

Summary

A study of rural church membership in the four counties reveals that membership varies widely from county to county, apparently in keeping with the socio-economic status of the people. In Northumberland County where income is comparatively high, and home ownership and home life are on unusually high levels, the proportion of Negroes who are church members is 89.7 per cent. In Mississippi County where tenancy is high and home ownership and living standards are low, only about 10 per cent are church members.

While most churches report a small number of new members taken in annually, the net losses are larger, and over a period of years may be sufficient to reduce seriously the church's position and program. The losses are due mainly to migration, which at the present continues at a heavy rate in the rural South. In general, the rural ministry is not deeply disturbed at the exodus or its probable effects on the church.

The revival is still popular in the country, and bids fair to remain so. Records of membership are loosely kept, reflecting pastoral indifference and the limitations of the laity. Lack of records makes intensive follow-up of individual religious development difficult if not impossible. Noteworthy exceptions to the general weakness in handling members is found in the alumni clubs of several Northumberland County churches.

Chapter Five

CHURCH FINANCE

The study of rural church finances revealed some gratifying as well as disturbing facts. Gratifying is the fact that rural people give generously to their churches. In the four-county study it was found that in 1944, the total amount contributed by 17,062 members of 107 churches in the year preceding the study was $87,397.00, a per capita contribution of $5.12. This is somewhat in excess of the national per capita figure for the Negro church as a whole, which according to the last census was $4.91.

As Table VI shows, the per capita contribution varied considerably from county to county. In Dallas County with an average church membership of 107, it was $4.18; in Calhoun, where the average membership is 188, it was $4.97. In Northumberland County where the average membership is highest, 431, the per capita contribution was $5.79. On the other hand, in Mississippi County where the average church membership is smallest, 81.4, the contribution was highest of all, $7.11, or 18.6 per cent higher than it was found to be in Northumberland County.

TABLE VI
Per Capita Contributions of Rural Church Members in Four Selected Counties

County	Number of Members	Amount Contributed	Per Capita Contribution
Calhoun	5,821	$28,929.00	$4.97
Dallas	5,571	23,280.00	4.18
Mississippi	1,790	12,728.00	7.11
Northumberland	3,880	22,460.00	5.79
All Counties	17,062	$87,397.00	$5.12

1. The national per capita contribution for the Negro church is $4.91. (Derived by dividing the total expenditure of the Negro church by the number of members.)

2. The national Negro rural per capita contribution is $3.69.

At least two interesting conclusions are suggested by these figures:

1. Members of some very small churches give proportionately more than members of larger churches. This, quite obviously, is due to the fixed expenses of church maintenance that must be met by the congregation whether it be large or small. If the membership is small, as has already been indicated in the preceding chapter, the fixed expenses require larger individual contributions.

2. In general, however, per capita contributions tend to increase with increasing size of church membership.

If Mississippi County with its uniformly small churches be excepted as a case out of the ordinary, it is seen that Northumberland County with its average membership of 431 has a per capita contribution of $5.79, which is 14.2 per cent higher than Calhoun County with an average membership of 188, and 27.6 per cent higher than Dallas County with an average membership of 107. The increase is not in direct proportion, however, for while the Northumberland average membership is more than four times as great as that of Dallas, Northumberland's per capita contribution is only one and one-fourth times as great.

The per capita figure found in this study is considerably above the national figure for Negro rural churches. This is true for each county. The national rural figure is $3.69,[1] but the average figure for the four counties is $5.12, and that for each county is $4.97, $4.18, $5.79, and $7.11 for Calhoun, Dallas, Northumberland, and Mississippi Counties respectively. Possibly one reason for the difference is that the 1936 national religious census was taken in the heart of the depression, when wages and farm income were much lower than at the time this study was made, 1944. If this is the reason for the present high contributions, then it indicates that rural people give increasingly as they have more to give. It may also be due to a more effective method of raising funds that is now in general use in the rural South (see below).

Business Methods

Only in Northumberland County was the budget system of handling church finances in general use. In this county all the ministers except one conducted the financial affairs of their churches according to an annual budget. The one who did not gave as his reason, "I don't like to count chickens before they hatch."

Northumberland County was the striking exception, how-

[1] *Religious Bodies*: 1936, Vol. I, p. 76. Washington, D. C., United States Department of Commerce, Bureau of the Census.

ever, in this regard. Two ministers in Mississippi County, seven in Calhoun, and none in Dallas used the budget plan. The use of an annual budget requires, of course, considerable thought and planning in handling the business affairs of the church. It means that a year's financial program must be envisioned beforehand, responsibilities allocated, and expenditures proportioned for the greatest good of the church. Yet only eighteen out of 114 churches used this simple, necessary means of conducting their financial affairs. In 84.2 per cent of the churches, affairs were carelessly and unsystematically handled, practically on a hit or miss basis.

The most common reasons given by the pastors for lack of system in administering church finances are:

1. The budget system is too complicated for rural congregations. The people cannot understand it.

2. The people do not appreciate much care in money matters. Many regard exactitude as an intimation of dishonesty.

3. The financial side of rural church work is so simple and so meager that it requires little planning or system.

While there is some truth in these statements, they still do not relieve pastoral leadership of its responsibility in the careful handling of church funds. Certainly over a period of time people could be trained in the simpler elements of sound business methods. More accurate reasons for the lack of system in rural church finances appear to be:

1. The absentee pastor. Ministers are not with their people long enough to direct them in sound monetary procedures.

2. In many cases the ministers are not able to direct the people. They lack knowledge and appreciation of good methods.

Here is clearly a great opportunity for guidance to which the church is not awake. When it is remembered that much of the exploitation characterizing the tenant system is perpetuated through the tenant's financial ignorance, we realize that any instruction in sound financial methods would be a training of great practical value. Also, when it is considered that the rural Negro's income is small and that the contribution he makes to his church represents a proportionately large and costly share of his income, it seems only fair, to say nothing of honest, to handle these funds with accuracy.

The Raising of Funds

In raising their funds most Negro country churches still adhere to the time-worn Sunday offering and special rally. They hold to these in spite of the fact that more effective methods such as the Lord's Acre and the Church Farm are rapidly coming into general use. One of these plans, the Lord's Acre, has literally revolutionized the financing of rural churches. Recognizing that country people may not have much money to give to their church, the plan permits them to give such things as they do have—the produce from a plot of land, or an animal, or a fowl, or the income from a period of work, anything that can be set aside in the name of the church. The plan not only increases church funds manyfold, but it works wonders in building up a sense of stewardship and in giving all members a chance for active participation in the life and work of the church.

Although most Negro pastors, either through ignorance or indifference, have been slow to employ the Lord's Acre method, throughout the South a small and increasing number of Negro rural churches are using it, and without exception they report excellent results from its use. One church in North Carolina has more than doubled its annual income. Two other churches in the same state, while not doubling their incomes, have greatly increased them. Since the plan has been so uniformly successful in helping needy churches to help themselves, many more rural churches should have the opportunity of trying it.[1]

The churches have developed a method, however, of increasing the size of their contributions that is now in general use throughout the four counties, and indeed the whole South. It is the plan of dividing the membership into groups or clubs, with a captain or leader appointed over each group. It is the duty of the leaders to collect church assessments or dues during the week days between services, and to turn in these funds with a written report on the "meeting Sunday." Generally each member is assessed or "supposed to give" a certain sum per month, usually fifty cents. This is used to pay the pastor's salary and most other fixed church expenses.

This method has not only increased contributions, but it has also considerably changed the nature of the country church collection. What formerly was a protracted period of begging and cajoling, if not unabashed scolding, lasting at times an hour or more, is now a rather quiet period of persons coming forward and reading names scribbled on scraps of paper. Unfortunately it is still as long as the old collection, and it still is a break in the continuity of worship. The reading of the names is often poorly done, and at best it is uninteresting. Therefore, throughout the whole process, people talk in low tones, or

[1] The Farmers Federation of Asheville, North Carolina, will freely furnish abundant information on the nature and use of the plan.

walk about the church. The procedure lacks the singing that formerly accompanied the collection, since singing interferes with the reading of the names.

The system appears to have these advantages:

1. It is partly a budgetary procedure in that every member is assigned a definite financial obligation. It does not apply, however, to the expenditure of moneys raised.

2. It permits each member to make his contribution, whether he attends service or not. More than any other thing, it has helped to offset the disastrous effect of bad weather on rural church services and finances. One often sees a large collection turned in at a service with few persons present.

3. The system has greatly increased the amount of money pastors actually receive. Heretofore the pastor's income was largely a book figure. What he received in cash was dependent upon the weather, the attendance at services, and such special efforts as the congregation would undertake. Now the pastoral obligations of a rural church can be met with much greater fullness and regularity.

Thus pastors with very small churches, some of which formerly would hardly have been able to meet the cost of pastoral transportation, are now able to pay a pastor all that is promised in the matter of salary, and to pay more for church maintenance than formerly was thought possible.

Pastors' Salaries

The amount paid by churches for pastoral services varied considerably, even within the same county. Thus, the highest annual amount paid in Calhoun County was $2,000, the lowest $72; in Northumberland County the highest was $1,500, the lowest $250. Table VII shows the total amount paid by the churches of each county, along with the highest, lowest, and average amounts.

TABLE VII
Amounts Paid by 107 Churches for Pastors' Salaries

County	County Total	Highest Salary	Lowest Salary	Average in County
Calhoun (31 churches)	$14,628.00	$2,000.00	$ 72.00	$471.87
Dallas (47 churches)	12,471.00	600.00	65.00	265.34
Mississippi (20 churches)	6,426.00	600.00	120.00	321.30
Northumberland (9 churches)	6,620.00	1,500.00	250.00	735.55
All Counties	$40,145.00			$375.19

The whole amount paid for pastors' services by 107 churches was $40,145.00, or an average figure of $375.19 per church. This figure means that 45.9 per cent, or nearly one-half of all moneys raised in rural areas went for pastors' salaries.

Fewer than one-fourth of the churches, 21.5 per cent, paid under $200 per year for pastoral salaries. Seventy-six of the 107 churches, 73.6 per cent, paid between $200 and $700 per year. Considering the fact that rural incomes are small, and congregations are also, the amounts devoted to pastoral salaries appear to be quite generous, especially in view of the very limited extent of pastoral service, which is mostly preaching, once or twice a month.

Few rural pastors have one church. Most have from two to four. As found in this study, the most common figure is two.

Table VIII indicates the number of churches held by each of eighty-four pastors. Only seven of these ministers served one church, forty-seven pastored two, twenty-seven pastored three, and three pastored four. Frequently a minister is encountered in the rural South who has five churches, and at the time of this study one minister in Virginia had seven.

TABLE VIII

NUMBER OF CHURCHES PER PASTOR IN FOUR SELECTED COUNTIES

CHURCHES PER PASTOR	CALHOUN COUNTY	DALLAS COUNTY	MISSISSIPPI COUNTY	NORTHUMBERLAND COUNTY	ALL COUNTIES
1 Church	2	1	0	4	7
2 Churches	17	17	10	3	47
3 Churches	7	17	3	0	27
4 Churches	0	3	0	0	3

The pastoring of more than one church is the chief means of increasing the rural minister's income. While few country churches individually are able to pay an adequate yearly salary, several of them together may give a pastor quite a respectable income. On the basis of this study, 87.5 per cent of rural pastors receive between $400 and $1,500 a year. The median salary is $650. There are reasons to believe, however, that throughout the South the yearly pastoral income of most rural ministers not only equals the median but tends to exceed it.

For instance, there appeared to be a general tendency for ministers to ask and for churches to pay not less than twenty-five dollars a month, or three hundred dollars a year, even for one Sunday's service a month. Where services were more frequent than once a month, salaries tended to increase. With the group plan of collecting church dues, it is now possible for churches to pay much more than formerly, when they were dependent mainly upon attendance on Sundays and at special rallies. Thus two churches each paying more than twenty-five dollars a month would take the pastor's income well above six hundred dollars a year.

Among Baptist churches particularly, the practice of observing a celebration each year, generally referred to in the country as the pastor's Anniversary, is a means of increasing considerably the pastor's income. The Anniversaries usually consist of a week of protracted meetings, during which the pastor is eulogized, testimonials of appreciation are expressed by neighboring churches, special programs are presented, and banquets are served. At the end the pastor receives an appreciation token, usually financial, which in many cases ranges between one and three hundred dollars. These contributions equal at times as much as one-third of a pastor's yearly salary. They serve to augment appreciably the amount a minister receives for his pastoral labors.

When the fact is considered that the rural pastor's work is largely confined to Sundays, and that he has most if not all of the remaining days of the week to spend in other lucrative occupations (see Chapter Eight), the general impression that the country preacher is grossly underpaid must be considerably revised. Only in the case where the rural pastor is resident and devotes his whole time to his church with no other source of income can he be regarded as underpaid. In accordance with the time he actually devotes to his parish, and in comparison with the average city pastor, most rural pastors are well paid, many are overpaid. The average country pastor devotes few days per month, besides Sundays, to parish work.

The urban minister is generally regarded as being at the call of his church every day.

Considering the time actually spent in rural work, the Negro rural pastor is considerably better paid than the Negro rural teacher.[1] Above all, he is free to supplement his church income with other kinds of work, which is not possible for most teachers.

Distribution of Funds

It was not possible to get accurate statements regarding the expenditure of rural church funds. The primary reason is the lack of account keeping in most rural churches.

Best reports of the division of expenditures were to be had from the Methodist churches, through reports made at their annual conferences. Yet even here a difficulty was encountered, for in many years the conference minutes are not printed, and some of those that have been printed do not give detailed financial statistics.

Among the Baptist churches, minutes of annual association meetings are sometimes printed, but frequently they do not show all amounts reported, nor do they divide the sums reported into separate items. Thus a church will "represent" in an association meeting with ten or fifteen dollars which is its contribution to education, home missions, foreign missions, and possibly other causes. As to how the fund is distributed, the minutes are often blank. Further, throughout the year rural churches make contributions to benevolent or general

[1] The average Negro teacher's salary in the rural South ranges between $300 and $700 per year. The average salary in Southern Negro elementary schools was $510 in 1935-36. *An American Dilemma,* by Gunnar Myrdal, Vol. I, p. 319. New York, Harper and Brothers, 1944.

causes of which no record is kept. Funds are raised in the services, often paid out in the services, and no permanent record is made of the transaction.

In nearly all cases it was difficult to find financial records covering any considerable period in the possession of one person or in one place. Since conference and association secretaries often change, sometimes annually, the transfer of records from an officer to his successor is often carelessly and incompletely done. It thus happens that significant records are lost, or widely scattered. The failure to find adequate financial records again revealed the loose and careless manner in which records as well as funds are handled in rural churches.

Of course, there were exceptions to this general statement. In Northumberland County, for example, two churches already referred to kept accurate financial records as well as membership and historical records. These cases are so exceptional, however, that they cannot be taken as representative of the entire study.

The 1943 and 1944 minutes of the Central South Carolina Conference of the African Methodist Episcopal Church, in which Calhoun County is located, were printed in excellent detail. Fifty-eight items of statistical value were recorded separately for each church, circuit (consisting of two churches), and mission, along with reports of presiding elders and other church officials or committees. Unfortunately, minutes of this calibre were not found elsewhere in the study, and in two counties no minutes were found at all.

Lacking records sufficiently general to justify even the most summary conclusions, recourse must be taken to the national figures of the United States census of religious bodies for an idea of the distribution of Negro church funds. Figures in the 1936 census show that Negro churches expended $23,669,940 for current expenditures and improvements, and $2,713,126, or 10.3 per cent, for missions and benevolences. This proportion of funds devoted to benevolences was considerably under the national figure for all churches, which was 17.0 per cent. According to the census, "the average Negro church contributed $1.00 for the larger interest of the organization for each $8.72 for maintenance. The ratio for all churches was $5.87 for local maintenance compared with $1.00 for benevolences and missions."[1]

These census figures apply to both rural and urban expenditures. By assuming that rural churches give proportionately as much as city churches, we are able to get something of a general impression as to the apportionment of funds in Negro rural churches, in the absence of more specific data.

The Keeping of Funds

Although each church had a treasurer or other officer chosen especially for keeping the church's funds, in not a single case was the financial officer bonded. With the smaller churches this is understandable, since funds raised are as a rule not very large, and also since most funds are raised as needed, and therefore are not on hand for long periods. But this is not true in many cases, particularly with the larger churches. Funds raised in rallies and through special efforts often run high into the hundreds of dollars, sometimes as high as one or two thousand dollars in cash.

That there is not greater financial loss in rural church funds

[1] *Religious Bodies*: 1936, Vol. I, p. 76.

is perhaps a tribute to the sincerity of laity as well as clergy. In one county a new church building costing twenty-seven thousand dollars was erected over a period of three years. The funds were raised as the church was built, and upon completion, the church was fully paid for. In all this period there was no question of loss or displacement of funds, and yet not one of the financial officers was bonded.

In spite of this record of financial faithfulness, it would seem wise to give rural churches the protection of guarantees against unexpected loss. Certainly any practice in sound financial methods is a needed element in the training of a handicapped people. Again this appears as an opportunity for the service-minded rural ministry.

Title to Church Property

One evident weakness of rural church administration was found in the matter of deeds to church property. More than one-fourth of one hundred and four churches, twenty-nine, either did not hold or were uncertain of their holding title to church property. Of the churches in Calhoun County, 6.5 per cent held no deeds to land or building; 21.0 per cent in Mississippi County, and 22.4 per cent in Dallas County, similarly held no title to their property. In addition, one church in Dallas County, three churches in Mississippi County, and nine churches in Calhoun County were uncertain as to whether there was a deed or not. That is to say, neither pastor nor any layman was able to tell if the church had ever held a deed. To make the matter worse, in cases where deeds were supposed to exist, it often happened that no one knew where the deed was. Church officers have changed, church leaders have died, and most vital church records have become lost in the changes.

This uncertainty and resulting confusion goes back to the founding of church groups, sometimes even back to pre-Emancipation times. In some cases a group of people desiring to establish a church would purchase land outright. In other cases a kindly landowner would simply set aside a plot of ground for the site of the colored church, sometimes with and sometimes without formal transfer of title. Where no title was transferred, it was generally understood that the right to use the land was permanent. As time passes, however, many factors enter to break the church's right to the land. Lands change hands, rural lands increase in value, lands formerly used for one purpose are later used for another. Thus a rural church that began with every promise of permanence and security even without title, may in time find itself in the midst of a changed situation, undesired and insecure, its very right to exist questioned.

A case in point was found in Dallas County, Alabama. A large church, formerly located on a cotton plantation, now stands closed and abandoned, in the midst of an open pasture range. Formerly the church stood in the center of a populous colored community. In recent years, the landholders have changed from cotton growing to cattle raising. Many of the members have moved to other sections, and those who remain now find themselves without a church. The landlord who holds title to the property has deliberately closed the church, and has barred its members from passing through his pasture. Some of his cattle have been affected with a contagious disease. He feels that the churchgoers passing through his fields spread the disease among his cattle. This may or may not be true, but with no title to the property the congregation is able to do little save to wait until time brings a more sympathetic landlord, with whom they may come to some agreement.

In two other cases colored churches are located on property desired for white residential settlement. Although one of the churches has been on its present site for fifty-three years, it can show no deed to its property, and it is now in fear of eviction with no compensation for its loss.

It is obvious that few things could be as destructive to a congregation's morale as the sudden loss of an investment accumulated over many years. Failure to secure and record a title over a period of years is an open indication of indifferent if not incompetent leadership.

Summary

The study of church finances in the present rural church reveals facts that are satisfactory and gratifying, but also other facts that are unsatisfactory and in need of improvement. It is seen that rural people give generously to the support of their churches, especially when their low economic status is considered. It is seen, too, that their gifts increase as they have more to give.

While some small congregations must give proportionately more to maintain their churches, in general contributions tend to increase with the size of the church and the general level of social and economic life in which the church is located. Rural congregations seem reluctant to lose their churches and make generous, almost heroic, efforts to maintain them.

Rural churches pay well for pastoral service, especially when the very limited extent of that service is taken into account. Upon the basis of time devoted to the work, most rural pastors are well paid. They earn proportionately more than city pastors, or rural school teachers. With their freedom to use much of their time in other lucrative activities besides preaching, the rural pastors' income does not need to be seen either as discouraging or unattractive.

In general, throughout the rural church the matter of keeping financial records is most unsatisfactory. Unless an improvement is made many a church's resources will continue to be wasted or ineffectively used. Such carelessness as was found was not only a cause of waste but also an invitation to dishonesty. The wonder is that not more was found.

The same may be said for titles to church property. The South is changing, land values and land uses are changing. Care should be taken that the rural church shall not lose through carelessness much of its holdings accumulated sacrificially through the years.

Responsibility for improvement in church finances rests with ministerial leadership. The leaders should take the initiative. Granted that many rural congregations may not at present appreciate sound methods in matters financial, bringing them into such knowledge and appreciation is a vital element in their training as well as in the stability of the rural church.

Little information was obtained on distribution of funds in the rural church, but figures for the whole Negro church indicate that the Negro church devotes proportionately about one-third less of its expenditures to missions and benevolences than does the church as a whole for the nation.

Chapter Six

ADULT PROGRAM

The throbbing heart-beat of a church's life is, of course, the worship or the "preaching" service. It is this service that expresses the religious interest of the congregation and that gives impetus to all the wider social efforts of the church. The character of the worship service is thus at once a key to the vigor of the church and to the efficiency of the pastor who serves the church.

The Number of Services

In rural churches we see at once that the chief trouble with the worship service is its infrequency.

As Table IX shows, only ten churches out of 108, or 9.3 per cent, have preaching services every Sunday in the month. Fifty-five of them, 51.0 per cent, have full services two Sundays a month, and 43, or 39.7 per cent, have full services but one Sunday per month. In other words, if the four-county study is indicative of general conditions, about 90 per cent of rural churches have full worship services only one or two Sundays a month.

TABLE IX

NUMBER OF SUNDAYS PER MONTH PREACHING SERVICES ARE HELD IN
108 RURAL CHURCHES

COUNTY	ONE SUNDAY PER MONTH	TWO SUNDAYS PER MONTH	FOUR SUNDAYS PER MONTH
Calhoun (31 churches)	3	22	6
Dallas (48 churches)	38	10	0
Mississippi (20 churches)	2	18	0
Northumberland (9 churches)	0	5	4
All Counties (108 churches)	43	55	10

Dallas County had the largest percentage of one-Sunday churches, thirty-eight out of forty-eight, 79.1 per cent. In contrast, Northumberland County had no church with only one preaching service a month.

Calhoun County had six and Northumberland County had four four-Sunday churches. For Northumberland this was four out of nine churches, or 44.4 per cent, the highest percentage of any county. Dallas and Mississippi Counties had no four-Sunday rural churches at all.

In all of the 108 churches except one the preaching services were regularly held in the mornings or afternoons. In only one case was the main service held on Sunday night. In twenty-one churches both morning and evening preaching services were held on the "meeting" Sundays.

The fact that approximately 90 per cent of rural churches have but two or fewer services per month bespeaks a great spiritual deficiency in the life of the county Christian. It also affects adversely the work of the rural pastor. It is a serious limitation to any intensive ministerial program, and it is a strain on the continuity of pastoral influence in the community. Providing a greater number of full worship services in the rural church is therefore a matter of pressing import to the welfare of the church.

Lay Services

It is not to be assumed, however, that nothing goes on in the rural church on the Sundays when no preaching services are held. A great deal happens. In most rural churches the Sunday school, conducted by laymen with little pastoral assistance in most cases, is held every Sunday. On the open Sundays devotional services with special programs are conducted by lay groups within the church, such as missionary societies or usher boards, or by outside groups such as lodges or schools or burial societies. The result is that the rural church is seldom closed on a Sunday.

From the ministry's point of view, this fact is significant. With pastoral services in 90 per cent of the churches on only one or two Sundays a month, and lay services on the other two or three Sunday mornings and many Sunday evenings besides, the proportion of lay activities is surprisingly high. It means that the rural church is in large measure a layman's movement. It raises the question as to whether the pastor's influence in the community does not rest on the deep, loyal respect that the people have for the office more than on his leadership and participation in the life of the community. This, too, is a matter worthy of serious thought.

Nature of the Services

Elaborate descriptions of contemporary rural church services have been made by Hamilton and Ellison, Johnson, and Mays and Nicholson.[1] While quite accurate in analysis and interpretation, the studies of these authors lay too much stress on the sermon, and not enough on other elements of the rural service. Mays and Nicholson, writing more than ten years ago, speak of the service as an "escape."[2] Today it is recognized that the escape hypothesis has been badly overdrawn. The rural church may provide its worshipers with emotional release and stimulation, and it may admonish patience in the face of trouble, but this is in no sense an escape from the problems of life. In fact, it is quite the opposite. It is learning to live with trouble, rather than to flee it.

In considering the minister's part as a leader of worship, it can be said at once that the Negro rural minister adheres closely in all essentials to the common American pattern. Neither the Negro minister nor the Negro rural church service he conducts have any strikingly peculiar characteristics. It has been shown conclusively and repeatedly that there are few if any distinctive elements in Negro religion.[3] The Negro received and developed his Christianity on American soil as part of the American Christian body. It would be strange indeed if his religion were different in any essential respects from the rest of American Christianity.

The untrained rural minister is naturally limited in his

[1] *The Negro Church in Rural Virginia*, by C. H. Hamilton and John M. Ellison. Bulletin No. 273, Virginia Agricultural Experiment Station, 1930.

Growing Up in the Black Belt, by Charles S. Johnson, pp. 137 ff. Washington, D. C., American Council on Education, 1941.

The Negro's Church, by Benjamin E. Mays and J. W. Nicholson, Chap. XIII. New York, Institute of Social and Religious Research, 1933.

[2] Mays and Nicholson, *op. cit.*, p. 249.

[3] *An American Dilemma*, by Gunnar Myrdal, Vol. II, pp. 937 ff. New York, Harper and Brothers, 1944.

theology, his world view, his thought of the nature and destiny of man. But his limitations are those that are common to all untrained ministers.

The untrained preacher depends heavily upon emotion in his preaching, and in order to make up for his lack of wider knowledge, lays stress upon doctrinal or emotional specialities such as a particular mode of baptism, an exclusive way of salvation, or the sin of dancing and playing cards. It is the untrained pastor who pays least attention to the daily needs and problems of his people, and it is against this kind of preaching that the inaccurate term "otherworldly" can most properly be directed.

As to methods of sermon delivery, the untrained rural pastor often makes the first half of his message a reading of some sermon that he has copied verbatim from a book, no matter how old or inapplicable the sermon may be. This part he calls, with a lack of humor, the "intellectual part." Since reading for these men is a difficult undertaking and therefore is ineffective, they try in the latter half of the message to make up for the poor first part by offering a heated hodge-podge of emotional shibboleths mixed with bits of common sense. Again, this is a common practice of all untrained ministers. The large numbers of books of sermons and sermon outlines sold in rural sections indicates that many if not most ministers in the South get their ideas and methods from minds other than their own.

In sharp contrast, the services conducted by trained Negro rural ministers are the equal of services by similarly trained men anywhere. This is to be expected. The trained minister's faith would be that of the denomination to which he belongs, and his methods would be those of other trained men in his group.

In practically every instance, it is the trained minister who has achieved most in the way of a pastoral program, and who is least dependent upon histrionic tricks and posing.

As has been previously said, most criticisms of rural church services center on the sermons. Since the great majority of rural ministers are untrained, their sermons are generally faulty, and can fairly be criticized at many points. This is particularly the case when the efforts of untrained men are judged in the light of highest standards. While much that is said is disparaging and is aimed at making the rural minister and his work appear ridiculous, the more thoughtful studies, such as the three mentioned above, are accurate and fair, and are based upon actual observations.

Most criticisms overlook entirely, however, the basic meaning and service of the sermon. In this sense, practically no study is appreciative or fully constructive. Critics point out the excess of emotion, the homely imagery, the faulty grammar, the limited theology, the crude anthropomorphisms, the heavenly reveries. They overlook entirely the nobility of the thing itself—a limited leader's effort to bring a limited people into communion with their God, an effort that may be weak in many ways, but never ridiculous. Poor as it is, the rural sermon is the community's only regular injunction to higher living. Out of six hundred sermons heard and analyzed, although many were crude and some were "otherworldly," not one failed to appeal for a higher life and greater godliness *in this world*.

Also, it ought to be said that even homeliness of language

and figure may have some virtue, particularly when a high purpose underlies them. Country people for the most part are simple, homely people. At least some phases of a message should be put into language they can understand and use. This is not to be taken, however, as an apology for ignorance in the rural pulpit.

Practically all criticisms of the rural sermon seem to assume that if preaching were better the people would be better. This overlooks the fact, verified in this study, that the effective element in improving people is not preaching, but programs; not eloquence, but leadership in the activities of everyday life.

It overlooks, too, the infrequency of the rural sermon, which perhaps does more to make rural preaching ineffective than the quality of the sermon. It is doubtful if any preacher, however eloquent or wise, could greatly affect the life of his people when he only sees and speaks to them once or twice a month. Non-residence does much more to weaken the influence of the country pastor than the character of the sermon he delivers.

The Conduct of Worship

Most rural church services are in many ways unsatisfactory. Their chief weaknesses are:

1. Late beginnings. Few rural services begin on time. Members seldom arrive on time. Services scheduled for eleven o'clock often begin at twelve or one. Even after arrival members stand around outside, and a protracted period of loud preliminary singing and praying is necessary to draw them into the church.

2. The lack of decorum throughout the service. Persons

noisily come into and go out of the church at all times, often during prayers. However, the increasing use of ushers in rural services, due to the rise and activity of usher boards (to be described later), is tending to discourage this practice.

3. Lack of preparation for the service. While most pastors follow a general order for the principal elements of the service, such as opening devotions, the several offerings, the sermon, the invitation to membership, introduction of visitors, and so on, the details of the service are not worked out beforehand. Especially is this true of untrained ministers. Persons who are to participate are asked to do so on the spur of the moment without chance for previous preparation; the responses as a rule are either too long or too short, often inappropriate, and consequently ineffective.

4. The injection of disturbing, personal elements into the service. Frequently improper personal references and scoldings are delivered from the pulpit, and in extreme cases open quarrels may be carried on. All of this is disastrous to any worshipful atmosphere.

5. The long, unworshipful manner of raising funds (see Chapter Five).

6. The tendency to regard violent emotion as the highest religious experience, and therefore the determination to produce such emotion at each service.

These are some of the leading weaknesses of most rural services. They reveal clearly the failings of the services, and the failings of the pastors in this particular. Almost always they are the result of lack of training, and therefore are characteristic of the untrained pastors. Indeed, the character of the worship service may be considered more directly indicative of the extent of training than any other aspect of rural church life.

These weaknesses are to be found in many rural churches, but they are not to be found in all. A few churches were found whose services begin on time. Several pastors evinced a keen appreciation of order, decorum, and preparation in the conduct of their services. Several pastors had overcome the disturbing ugliness of the collection. For example, in three churches in Northumberland County, offerings are made in envelopes deposited as plates are passed. One pastor in Calhoun County has the envelopes deposited at the door as persons enter the church.

In all cases except one, these were the achievements of trained men. It should be said, too, that a change to better methods is not easily or suddenly made. It is the result of education, and this as a rule takes time. The achievements of a few, however, are indications of what may be done by more. In short, improving rural worship need not be seen as an entirely hopeless undertaking.

Pastoral Visitation in Rural Parishes

Many phases of a minister's work cannot be carried on effectively without intimate, frequent contacts between the pastor and his people. Unfortunately, in this respect, as in rural worship, the ministry falls short of meeting the needs.

For example, thirty-one rural churches in Calhoun County were found to be receiving a total of only 68 days of pastoral visitation per month exclusive of the Sundays on which preaching services were held. This means that the rural parishes of that county received an average of 2.2 days of pastoral visiting monthly. The average does not mean, however, that every parish was visited by its pastor during the month, for six parishes received no visits at all from their pastors except "on call," that is, except when the pastor was specifically requested to come to the parish for some particular purpose, such as the illness of a member, or a funeral, or an extra service.

Mississippi County with an average of 2.8 pastoral visitation days a month was a little higher, and Dallas with an average of 4.0 was higher still. Northumberland was highest of all with an average of 15.4 days per month. On the other hand, twelve parishes in Dallas received no pastoral visits other than "on call," and likewise three parishes in Mississippi County.

As Table X shows, only three rural parishes out of forty-eight in Dallas County and three out of nine in Northumberland had resident, or full-time pastors. Calhoun County had one and Mississippi County had no parish receiving the pastor's full time.

TABLE X

NUMBER OF DAYS OF PASTORAL VISITING PER MONTH
RECEIVED BY 108 RURAL CHURCHES

COUNTY	TOTAL NUMBER OF DAYS	AVERAGE NUMBER OF DAYS PER CHURCH	PARISHES HAVING FULL TIME RESIDENT PASTORS
Calhoun (31 churches)	68	2.2	1
Dallas (48 churches)	190	4.5	3
Mississippi (20 churches)	55	3.0	0
Northumberland (9 churches)	139	15.4	3
All Counties (108 churches)	452	4.2	7

The following were the chief reasons given by the pastors for so little time spent in parish work:

1. Difficulties of travel caused by the war, especially the gasoline shortage.

2. The expense of frequent trips to the parish, which many said they could not afford, especially since their pay was so meager.

3. Outside work, which allowed the pastors little time for pastoral visiting.

Other causes were found, in addition to those given by the ministers, that also need to be taken into consideration:

1. The indifference of the laity toward pastoral visiting. In Chapter Eleven it is seen that many laymen do not expect their pastors to visit. They have little appreciation of the pastoral office other than that of preaching.

2. Similarly, the popular impression held by clergy and laity alike that the rural ministry is a preaching ministry; pastoring is secondary or incidental. This, of course, is a historic hangover from the old circuit riding days when a preacher's sole mission was to preach the word and win converts. This idea still holds firmly in the country, despite the modern change to the "station" or pastoral concept of the ministerial office. The result is that preaching in the city and country are not thought of in the same terms. For example, in six cases where individual ministers serve both urban and rural churches it was found that their attitudes toward their two charges is quite different. For the urban church pastoral visiting is planned as an essential part of the ministerial program. It is not regarded as equally necessary for the rural church, and therefore not as much of it is contemplated.

In other words, the pastor does not plan to do much visiting in the country, and the people do not expect it.

This lack of the pastor's presence in the rural community means that the families he serves are deprived of the intimate moral and religious guidance so necessary for progressive Christian living. For a people of Southern tenant and share-cropper status, handicapped in so many ways, this lack of fellowship and friendly counsel is tragic.

In spite of the reasons given by the ministers, it still seems that more of them could spend more time on their parish fields if they were minded to do so. Certainly the seventeen ministers mentioned in Chapter Eight who indicated that they have no work besides their pastorates, and who together spend a total of seventy-one days a month in the field, roughly four days per month per pastor or one day a week—certainly these men could give more time to their work. One day a week is very little for a membership that often runs up into the hundreds. Here again the average sounds better than the actual, for five of the seventeen ministers do no pastoral visiting except "on call."

Distance, while an inconvenience, is not necessarily an obstacle. As is shown in Table XI, approximately two-thirds of the pastors live within twenty miles of their charges, and nearly one-third live within ten. With present modes of travel, ten or twenty miles is not a great problem, even in time of war. If trips to the parish were carefully planned and visits were wisely grouped, it would still be possible for many more pastors to give more time to their people than they now do.

Perhaps a key to the possibility of greater pastoral visiting is to be found in the statement made by a minister belonging to one of the Methodist bodies in Calhoun County. When asked the reason for so little time spent in his parish, he replied: "I do a great deal of pastoral visiting coming up to conference." By this he meant that he found time for pastoral visiting when he had a special interest to promote. Perhaps he and other ministers could find more time to spend in their parishes if the impelling interest were to work intimately with their people.

When all the factors have been taken into account, it appears that the main reasons for the limited time spent by rural pastors in their parish fields are: (1) the pastors for various reasons do not plan to do much visiting, and (2) the rural laity do not expect it, and for that reason do not demand it.

Location of Pastoral Residences

Most rural pastors live away from their charges. Out of 108 churches, only fourteen pastoral residences were found to be located in the same community as the church. The remainder, ninety-four, were located from three to seventy miles away.

Table XI shows the distances between churches and pastoral residences for the four counties. In Northumberland County five out of nine pastoral residences, 55.6 per cent, were located in the same community as the church. Calhoun and Mississippi counties each had one such case, which amounted to 3.2 and 5.0 per cent respectively. In Dallas County seven out of forty-eight pastoral residences, 14.6 per cent, were located at or near their churches.

TABLE XI

DISTANCE OF PASTORS' RESIDENCES FROM 108 RURAL CHURCHES IN FOUR SELECTED COUNTIES

COUNTY	NUMBER OF RESIDENCES LOCATED IN CHURCH COMMUNITIES	NUMBER OF RESIDENCES LESS THAN 10 MILES FROM CHURCH	NUMBER OF RESIDENCES BETWEEN 10 AND 20 MILES FROM CHURCH	AVERAGE DISTANCE OF RESIDENCE FROM THE CHURCH	GREATEST DISTANCE OF RESIDENCE FROM CHURCH
Calhoun (31 churches)	1	8	17	16.1 Mi.	70 Mi.
Dallas (48 churches)	7	14	14	12.3	44
Mississippi (20 churches)	1	7	7	14.8	37
Northumberland (9 churches)	5	2	1	13.2	21
All Counties	14 12.9%	31 28.7%	39 36.1%		

Thirty-one of the 108, or 28.7 per cent, were located between three and ten miles away, and thirty-nine, or 36.1 per cent, between ten and twenty miles away. If the last two figures are added, it is seen that seventy churches, or 64.8 per cent, are between three and twenty miles away from their pastors' homes. The most extreme case was that of a pastor who lived seventy miles from his church, which, surprisingly, was a four-Sunday church.

Three reasons were found for pastors living away from their churches:

1. The multiple pastorate. Many rural pastors have two or more churches. They can only live near one.

2. The common practice of calling or assigning ministers to charges where they are neither expected nor required to live, which again, is a hangover from the circuit riding days.

3. The reluctance of many rural pastors to live among their folk. This reluctance is based upon the feeling that it is harder for a pastor to work with rural people when they know very much about his private life. It is felt that rural people respect and love most the pastor about whom they know least. As one pastor in Calhoun County expressed it: "It doesn't pay to let your people peep your hand"—an expression that comes, incidentally, from the card table!

The impression that rural people won't respect a pastor whom they know can be easily invalidated on many grounds. For instance, it is the qualities of the minister himself and not the place where he lives that determines the respect people have for him. Or, as was found in this study, it is the resident pastor who is most fully successful in his work. Perhaps by being respected the reluctant pastors are thinking of being idolized or lionized. It is quite possible that the tendency to idolize a person diminishes as intimacy grows. But posing as an idol should have no place in a truly Christian ministry. Although the impression is invalid and in actuality is groundless, it still is real and prevalent, and works to keep a large number of ministers from living among their people even where they can conveniently do so.

It has been shown above that the distance most rural ministers live from their parishes need not be a barrier to pastoral visiting. It needs to be clearly recognized that a non-resident ministry is a separated ministry, and that separation is a detriment to intimate pastor-people relationships. It must be hard to depend upon a pastor who is always ten, twenty, or more miles away. It is one of the reasons why so few laymen turn to their pastors for advice or help in some of the most vital matters of life (Chapter Eleven). Granting that rural people need quite as much spiritual attention as any other people, it is the responsibility of the rural ministry to see that they get it—a responsibility that the rural ministry at the present time is poorly bearing.

Church Organizations

The work of a church is largely dependent upon the extent to which the church is organized. The nature and extent of this organization is primarily the pastor's responsibility, and therefore is indicative of the pastor's efficiency.

The regular or customary church organizations are to be found in most rural churches, especially the organizations that are characteristic of the denomination to which the church belongs. Among Methodist churches there are the boards of trustees, stewards, stewardesses, deaconesses, and missionary societies; and among Baptists, boards of deacons, church aid groups, and missionary societies. These organizations are of course charged with the routine business and activities of the church, and hence are found in all country churches, even the smallest. In the larger and more active churches these groups often have branches among the younger people, generally known as junior groups.

Special Purpose Organizations

It is in the special purpose organizations, that is, organizations established to render some needed service to the church or to the community, that the rural church is most lacking. For instance, at the time of the study, only the churches in Northumberland County had regular meetings for the men of the church besides the official boards. In the other three counties no church was found that had organized the men into special interest groups, such as civic clubs, father and son clubs, craft clubs, recreation clubs, and the like.

Only one church out of 108 had a literary club, a club whose purpose was to stimulate interest in good reading. Only one had a study club, a club whose aim was improving the practical as well as the academic knowledge of the people of the community. Four churches of the 108 had mothers' clubs; three held community meetings, that is, meetings like public forums for discussing matters of community and national interest. Three churches had circulating libraries, or more accurately, stocks of books that the members could borrow for home use.

In the face of the needs of the rural Negro, this paucity of special service activities by the rural church is not merely a weakness, it is a shame. It is a direct result of the untrained and the absentee pastor, and of negative pastoral attitudes. Responsibility for it falls on the denomination as well as on the individual pastor. For instance, the frightful rate of Negro infant mortality in the Mississippi Delta area has been pointed out often. What more effective attack on the problem could be made than to give the mothers of the area a sense of the sacredness, the beauty, the responsibility of motherhood, along with the practical knowledge motherhood needs? This psychological or spiritual improvement is quite as necessary as economic improvement, and must go along with it if rounded progress is to be made. Yet in Mississippi County in the heart of the delta not a single mothers' club was to be found in any rural church.

The Negro tenant lives under oppressive forces that tend

to break his spirit as well as his back. His spiritual plight is fully as severe as his economic, social, or political plight. Yet, not a single church in the lower Southern counties of this study had any kind of organized activity to combat the spiritual depression and atrophy.

Accepting the lack of training of the rural minister as the cause for his inactivity, this leaves wholly inexplicable the lack of activity on the part of trained people at the head of denominational bodies who could plan and put into effect programs of special service that would do much to lift the whole tone of rural life, and to make the church a more vital rural instrument.

Usher Boards

One of the most prevalent, most active and most popular of rural church organizations is the Usher Board. Organized ostensibly to provide members to serve as ushers at services, these groups have rapidly taken on the nature of church or community clubs. They have junior and senior branches, but often the old and the young meet together without distinction. The boards conduct weekly "sings" to which groups from other churches are invited; they present programs in the churches on Sundays in which other boards join; they promote activities to raise money for the church and for charities among their members; many of them give social or recreational affairs that are quite popular in many communities. During the offering in the Sunday services, the usher board members make their contribution as a group, marching by the collection table in rhythmic single file, singing as they deposit their offerings. These groups in many communities attract more young people than any other church organization. Organized to render a specific church service, they soon engage in a much wider range of activities. They apparently are a homely effort on the part of the laity to meet the lack of social and community activities in the church.

Summary

In looking at the adult program of the rural church it is seen that nine-tenths of rural churches have only half or less than half as many services per month as churches in the cities. This means that the rural Christian gets not only a diminished share of preaching, but also a diminished share of pastoral guidance and inspiration in meeting the problems of his daily life.

The small amount of pastoral leadership throws much religious activity upon the laymen of the community. While this is a credit to lay leadership, it is neither a credit nor an advantage to the ministry. It means that dependence upon the ministry is lessened, and too much of this may come to mean lessened respect for the pastoral office.

While the rural pastor in visiting his parish may have some difficulties the urban pastor does not have to face, the difficulties are not insurmountable. When all the reasons have been taken into account, it still seems that more rural pastors could and should spend more time with their charges.

The number of special service organizations in the rural church is an index to the wider service the church renders its people and its community. Such organizations are very few, and consequently the number of vital services rendered by the rural church is very small. This is a matter deserving the immediate consideration of individual pastors and denominational bodies as well, for it affects not only the local parish, but the future of the Christian church.

How long the country Christian will continue to support a ministry whose primary function is to bring a thrill once or twice a month is of course an open question. It is only reasonable to assume that the rural Christian some day will question the extent to which his ministry is helping to lift him up into the more abundant life. And upon the answer to that question will depend his loyalty to the church in his community and his faith in Christianity as a whole.

Chapter Seven

THE YOUNG PEOPLE'S PROGRAM

Of all the activities of the rural church, perhaps none is more important than that of touching its young—of giving them knowledge of the Christian religion, and of providing wholesome interests and activities to guide their growth in the Christian life. The child as part of the rural family is an integral element in the rural church. And the child's development is the foundation and hope of continuation of the church. It is the purpose of this chapter to determine the extent to which the rural church is meeting the demands of this vital phase of its work.

The Rural Sunday School

All rural churches have church schools, or Sunday schools, as they are still generally termed in the country. Most of them meet every Sunday, and as Mays and Nicholson affirm, they are second in importance only to the preaching services.[1]

Because most ministers live away from their parishes, the

[1] *The Negro's Church,* by Benjamin E. Mays and J. W. Nicholson, p. 254. New York, Institute of Social and Religious Research, 1933.

responsibility of instructing the young falls largely upon rural laymen. The faithfulness with which the laymen promote and conduct the country Sunday school is a noble instance of Christian loyalty and a great service to the Christian church. For without this persistent faithfulness in the face of pastoral absence and inefficiency, the propagation of the Christian religion among rural youth would be seriously endangered.

But this effort, which from one point of view is so noble and so essential, is beset with a great number of practical handicaps that nobility of spirit alone cannot overcome.

The Size of the Rural Sunday School

Table XII shows the size of 105 rural Sunday schools in the four counties. For the most part, the schools are small. Six schools had but five members or less; twenty-six had between eleven and twenty members, and fifty-three or half of the 105 ranged between twenty and fifty members. In other words, more than three-fourths, 86.7 per cent, of the Sunday schools studied had fifty or fewer members.

Theoretically the small school should have its advantages as well as its disadvantages. Smallness should make possible more intimate, more intensive instruction. But since rural Sunday school teachers generally are poorly prepared, as is seen below, the advantages seldom become realities. It was found that mostly the disadvantages of smallness accrue to the rural Sunday school.

For example, division into grades or departments was least satisfactory in the small school. Since the number of scholars in the school is small, it is difficult to break them up into

TABLE XII

NUMBER OF SCHOLARS IN 105 RURAL SUNDAY SCHOOLS

NUMBER OF SCHOLARS	NUMBER OF SUNDAY SCHOOLS				
	Calhoun County	Dallas County	Mississippi County	Northumberland County	All Counties
1– 5	0	4	2	0	6
6–10	2	3	1	0	6
11–20	9	11	6	0	26
21–25	1	3	6	0	10
26–40	9	12	3	1	25
41–50	4	10	1	3	18
51–60	1	1	0	0	2
61–75	1	0	0	0	1
76–99	0	0	0	2	2
100–	4	2	0	3	9
Number of Sunday schools in each county	31	46	19	9	105

still smaller divisions with only one or two children in a class. A superintendent in Dallas County stated that it is hard enough to get adults to work with large groups. He felt he never would be able to get them for classes of one or two.

Secondly, facilities tend to be poorer in the smaller schools. It was found that literature, charts, pictures, and so on were least satisfactory where the schools were smallest. This was due to the fact that small schools have small incomes. In most rural churches the Sunday school is self-supporting. To meet financial demands that exceed the Sunday offerings, special drives or efforts are made by the leaders of the school. In only fourteen cases was religious education, which means mainly the Sunday school, found to be included in the financial program of the rural church. Needless to say these were churches where budgeting or some sort of financial planning was followed. In all other cases, the Sunday school raised its own funds and provided the materials for its work. Under such a practice the small school suffers.

Thirdly, enthusiasm is lowest in the small school. This is true for both leaders and scholars. Children are more attracted to a large, thriving activity than they are to a small, although thorough one. Adults are less willing to give their time to a small enterprise, as was mentioned above.

There are striking exceptions, however. In Mississippi County a Sunday school was found that had five children, all of them from two families. The teacher was a college graduate, the wife of a farmer and a teacher in the local public school. She met her pupils faithfully each Sunday, and provided some measure of instruction and activity for each, although no two were on the same age level. In another case, the chief activity in a small Sunday school was the adult Bible class. It consisted of only seven elderly people, but they met each Sunday with great regularity, and their discussions of doctrine and biblical interpretation were most enthusiastic.

The Teaching Program

One index to the character of teaching done in the rural Sunday school is found in the number of grades into which the school is divided. Grades indicate not only instructional divisions, but also activities suited to the needs of the child on his age and intelligence level.

The number of grades of 106 Sunday schools is shown in Table XIII. Seven schools had only one grade for all pupils. Twenty-two schools had two grades, and thirty-nine had

TABLE XIII
NUMBER OF GRADES IN 106 RURAL SUNDAY SCHOOLS IN FOUR SELECTED COUNTIES

COUNTY	1 GRADE	2 GRADES	3 GRADES	4 GRADES	5 GRADES	MORE THAN 5 GRADES
Calhoun	4	7	10	7	1	1
Dallas	2	14	24	7	0	0
Mississippi	1	1	5	6	6	1
Northumberland	0	0	0	5	4	0
All Counties	7	22	39	25	11	2

three. The three-grade school was quite the most common. Twenty-five schools were divided into four grades, and thirteen into five or more. If the two- and three-grade types are added, they constitute more than half, 57.5 per cent, of all schools.

Because of the small size of most rural Sunday schools, the division into grades is not adequate for effective teaching. For instance, in the two-grade school the scholars are divided into "Children" and "Adults"; or "Beginners" and "Advanced" or "Bible Class." Beginners include children from three or four years up to eight or ten; the Advanced range from eight to sixteen or eighteen. Adults or Bible Class members are usually mature persons interested in religious learning, but frequently one or two bright youngsters may be included among them, particularly if the young ones can read and are not inclined to lord their academic advantage over the more limited adults.

The Sunday schools with four grades or more are found among the larger and more enlightened churches, and as a rule are organized according to the standards of religious education in the denomination to which the church belongs.

[111]

The following description of a session of a two-grade Sunday school is fairly typical of the smaller schools: there were only four adults among the twenty-one scholars present, and since they preferred to remain in the children's group only one class was held, instead of the usual two. The youngsters ranged in age from a boy of four to a boy of sixteen and a girl of seventeen, both in high school. The group was taught by two elderly persons, the teacher and the leader, or resource person. Quarterly leaflets published by the denomination were used. It was said that each child had been given a leaflet at the beginning of the quarter, but since most of them had left these at home, there were but four on hand, and they were passed from person to person as each read aloud.

The method of teaching was simple. The teacher would call upon an older child or an adult to read the golden text, the memory verse, or a paragraph from the lesson. In general the reading was poor, and the pronunciation of biblical terms was embarrassing. At the end of each reading, the teacher would ask what was the meaning of something that had been read. The adults, either because they did not know, or perhaps to give the youngsters a chance, remained silent. The children invariably said they did not know, or just negatively shook their heads when the instructor looked in their direction. Getting no response from the class, the teacher would then turn and ask the leader for the answer. He, with good faith but little knowledge, was always ready to explain elaborately. In answer to the question "Who were the Gentiles?" he replied that they were white people, and to "Who were the Pharisees?" he answered, "They are anybody that's mean and don't love the Lord."

A number of significant conclusions are to be drawn from this typical Sunday morning experience in a rural community. First, most of the young people were in the upper grammar and high school grades. The Sunday school's methods of teaching and the capability of the teachers was in sad contrast to prevailing educational standards even in a rural Southern school. How long the young people will witness the contrast and keep their respect for the religious school is a question for earnest consideration.

Secondly, in this Sunday school there was nothing for the small children to do—nothing to increase their knowledge of God or his love or his world. The little boy of four and three other children not much older sat with amazing quietness through most of the lesson. One little fellow talked quietly to himself as if his mind were moving in another world, quite oblivious to all that was going on about him. With the older children admitting that they did not know, and no instruction for the young, one may well wonder about the security of the foundation on which these young people must build their Christian faith and their lives. It should be said, however, that when methods of more effective teaching were suggested, along with ways of bringing the children themselves into fuller participation in both the teaching and learning processes, the teachers and adults responded most favorably. They were quick to admit that what they need now is knowledge, both of subject and of method.

In this Sunday school no minister or other person trained in religion is regularly present. The minister attends on the preaching Sundays, twice a month, but the teachers stated that he could do little to improve the Sunday school work.

Not every small Sunday school uses a teacher and a leader, but the method of reading, explaining, and commenting upon what is read, and sometimes memorizing the Bible verse, constitutes the teaching routine.

It is customary at the conclusion of the session in a general assembly for some adult, usually the pastor when he is present, to review or summarize the lesson of the day. One hundred and four pastors out of 108 indicated that the review is a major part of their participation in the Sunday school. Twelve pastors give blackboard demonstrations in making the review. Over half of the 108 pastors, 63, stated that they also teach classes when present.

The Training of Sunday School Leaders

Considering the question of teachers and teaching, it can be said at once that the rural church is well aware of the need of better trained teachers. In response to the question "Are the teachers in your Sunday school trained?" only 14 ministers out of 88 answered that they were. Sixty-two, or 70.5 per cent, said definitely that they were not. Twelve stated that their teachers had some training, but not nearly as much as was needed for efficient work.[1] When it is remembered that many ministers are themselves untrained in religious education methods and that consequently their standards are low, it makes more questionable the quality as well as the number of those listed as being trained.

The opinions of the ministers regarding the efficiency of

[1] *Training* as used here means not only academic training but also any study in religious education, such as is offered in short courses, Sunday school conventions, or even through correspondence courses.

their teachers was somewhat more encouraging than their opinions on training. Twenty-five out of 86 ministers felt that their teachers were efficient despite the fact that many of them had had no training. Thirty-five were positive their teachers were not efficient, while 26 regarded their teachers as fairly so. But here again the statements of the ministers had to be qualified in two respects: first, in their conception of efficient religious teaching which in most cases was poor; and secondly, by their tendency, in spite of caution, to confuse efficiency with faithfulness. It was very hard for most ministers to class a person who served earnestly and regularly as an inefficient teacher.

To check further on the pastor's awareness of the efficiency of his Sunday school, ninety ministers were asked if they felt that their young people were getting the fundamentals of the Christian religion. Thirty-five ministers said that they were, thirty-five said they were not, and twenty said they were getting something of the fundamentals but not enough. In putting the question it was stated that fundamentals included knowledge of the Bible, the life of Christ, and basic church doctrines. The pastor's own knowledge of these items, of course, determined to some extent his conception of how much his young people were getting.

As a summary test pastors were asked to state what they felt was the chief need in the religious instruction of their young people. Of the ministers replying, about three-fourths, 74.5 per cent, stated that the main need was better trained teachers. A few added that in addition to technical training a deeper sense of consecration was needed in those who taught. Five said that Sunday school teachers need more religion.

In order of frequency the chief needs in religious education were said to be:

better trained teachers
more knowledge of the Bible
more teaching of church doctrines
more consecration in teachers
more religion in teachers
more exemplary living by teachers and adults
more social knowledge
better Sunday school literature

Only one minister stated that his young people were in need of "nothing in particular."

With three-fourths of the ministers calling for better trained teachers, it is clear that the rural ministry is aware of the ineffectiveness of current religious education. But what the ministry is doing or plans to do about it is another matter.

Pastoral Instruction of Teachers

Only thirty-nine ministers out of seventy-four were found to have instruction classes for their teachers. Twenty-nine hold no such classes at all, while six ministers speak about the matter in their sermons or to the teachers as a group at infrequent intervals.

Many Sunday school workers go to teachers' institutes, summer short courses, or Sunday school conventions conducted by their denominations, but they go through their own initiative and by their own efforts, with little active pastoral assistance. Only six out of 108 pastors of churches indicated an *active* interest in helping their Sunday school workers to become better trained.

The only reasons deducible for pastoral inactivity in the face of such an obvious need are the two handicaps so often met before in this study: first, lack of training, and second, non-residence.

Since many rural ministers are untrained both academically and in the techniques of their profession—of which teaching the young is one—they are not equipped to meet a need that exists before their eyes. Also, since they are seldom in their parishes, the opportunity to hold special meetings with their teachers is missed. The preaching Sunday is usually filled with church business and adult affairs, and affords little time for instruction in how to teach youth.

Most denominations have activities that aim to improve Sunday school teaching. Regular courses of study are offered by individual church bodies or by national agencies, such as the International Council of Religious Education. Regional directors of religious education are employed by various denominations, who conduct institutes and short courses in their areas. Sunday school conventions that are held annually, usually in the summer months, offer some systematic instruction to Sunday school workers. But with the exception of the conventions, these activities do not yet reach the rural teachers sufficiently. And it is to be remembered that practically half of the Sunday school membership of the Negro church is still in the country.[1]

While these activities aim to aid teachers, little is being done to help the minister. He is in immediate need in two ways: (1) in appreciation of the importance of adequate re-

[1] *Religious Bodies*: 1936, Vol. I, pp. 861 ff. Washington, D. C., United States Department of Commerce, Bureau of the Census.

ligious education according to modern standards, and (2) in the techniques of effective instruction. Since a limited ministry can hardly help itself, the general church bodies will have to take the lead. It seems fair to assume that there will be little improvement in this vital area of church life until the ministry has become more capable of offering the leadership it ought to give.

Young People's Literature

One minister expressed dissatisfaction with the character of the literature used in his Sunday school. His complaint was that it was not visually attractive to young people, and that the material of the lessons was not presented in forms suited to the life-needs of young people.

Although he was alone in voicing this feeling, it seems well taken. The leaflets used by most churches in the country are printed in small, closely packed type with few pictures or other illustrations. Applications of the lessons are on the adult level, and have little relation to the life of the child. Above all, the lessons contain few suggestions for *activities* by the Sunday school class, and it is now agreed that learning by doing is the most effective way of teaching religion as well as other things.

Mays and Nicholson pointed out in 1933 that the lesson material was wholly lacking in references to rural life, and had little relation to the life experience of the rural child. The lack of wholesome stories and inspirational fiction for young people was then and continues to be a serious deficiency.

The production of fitting literature that can be used in the country is one project to which denominational publishing houses with large rural circulations can devote themselves with especial fitness at this time.

Young People's Organizations

Nearly all of the larger rural churches have the young people's societies common to their denominations. Among Baptists these societies are Baptist Training Union groups, and among Methodists they are Christian Endeavor Societies, Epworth Leagues, and Methodist Youth Fellowship groups. Out of eighty-nine churches visited, fifty-six had these organizations.

In addition to the regular societies many ministers reported local young people's groups organized around some need in the church. It has already been mentioned that church boards and missionary societies often have junior branches (see Chapter Six). Junior churches were found in eight cases, junior usher boards in eleven, pulpit aid societies in three, and Royal Ambassadors in two churches pastored by the same minister. The chief function of these last seemed to be to help raise money for the church.

The vitality of such organizations, like that of the Sunday school, is dependent upon the type of leadership they have. But to a greater extent even than the Sunday school, they are the products of lay sponsorship and interest. In these organizations the young people are older and more inquisitive. Consequently, it is to them that the untrained pastor offers least guidance.

The greatest lack in the rural church's work with youth is the absence of special organizations having some service aim other than the specific needs of the church. Not a single church outside Northumberland County reported a study club, a discussion club, a hobby club, or any kind of recreational organization. In Northumberland County two churches had study or discussion societies for their young people. Four churches out of 108 reported that 4-H Clubs had been organized among their young people, and met regularly at the church. No church had a Boy or Girl Scout Club; none had teams for games of any kind. No church had a week-day program for its young people. None had supervised play or recreational activities at the church. The lack of play facilities for young people on the grounds of the rural church has already been mentioned (see Chapter Three).

The significance of this lack of activities is obvious. The life of the Negro farmer is dull and impoverished, as has already been shown, and is lacking in many of the elements that go to make an acceptable standard of living. The life of young people consequently suffers. Outside the public school, they have little chance to learn even the simple amenities of wholesome living. The church could render an enormous service here by giving its young people at least some measure of training in the beauty and dignity and joy of the decent life. At the present time, however, the rural church is not doing so. The rural school, like the urban school, aspires to work with the whole child. But the whole child has many parts, all of which need to be served. It is no credit to the church that some of its major functions are being taken over by other agencies because of the church's ignorance or indifference.

The responsibility for action in this realm rests with the ministry. The laity, while willing, are limited. Leaders must bring to the laymen the knowledge that they need. The chief leader of rural adults is still the rural minister.

Commercialized Amusements

In only six cases out of 108 did the pastors state that commercial amusements were a problem with their young people. These statements could mean: (1) that many of the vicious, commercialized activities such as drinking places, gambling houses, road houses, and the like have not yet invaded country communities to a great extent; or (2) that the young people who are members of churches or Sunday schools are less inclined to indulge in such activities; or (3) that the ministers, chiefly because of the little time spent on their parish fields, are not aware of conditions among their young.

Johnson finds that commercialized and illicit activities are beginning to attract rural youth, even where they must go into nearby towns to indulge.[1] But when due allowance is made for the possibility of error in the judgment of the pastors, it still seems unlikely that pastors of 102 churches out of 108 would be uniformly mistaken. The fact seems to stand that most of the young people connected with the church are not yet given to widespread indulgence in commercialized or unwholesome amusements. Here is a great opportunity for the rural church to fill the lives of its young people with wholesome, interesting, Christian activities, which after all are the surest bulwark against the attraction of injurious commercialized attractions.

[1] *Growing Up in the Black Belt,* by Charles S. Johnson, Chapter VI. Washington, D. C. American Council on Education, copyright 1941.

Summary

Work with rural youth is a most vital phase of the church's program. At present it is a work carried on for the most part by the laity, who have set themselves to it with noble spirit. The work, however, is beset with many handicaps and contains vast deficiencies. This is true both of the teaching process and of the activities conducted by the church for the development and guidance of the young. Teachers are limited in knowledge and ability, and ministers are limited in knowledge and in the time they give to the work.

While ministers are aware of the need, they are able to do little, because of their limited training, to improve prevailing conditions. Instruction of both preachers and people is imperative. It will have to come largely from trained persons who are willing to undertake the task of improving religious education in the country.

At the present time the rural church enjoys both the loyalty and respect of most of its young people. How long it will hold them depends upon the capacity of the church to act. At the conclusion of the most elaborate study yet made of the relation of rural youth to the church, Johnson writes:

. . . All evidence points to the conclusion that the church will increasingly influence youth as its programs take their needs into account on a new and improved cultural level. Where this has been done, the church has tended to retain its role as a vital social and spiritual force in molding the wholesome and socially acceptable patterns of behavior.[1]

[1] *Ibid.*

Chapter Eight

MINISTERIAL PREPARATION

Academic Training

In the four counties of this study eighty pastors of rural churches were interviewed on the question of their preparation. Of this number, thirty-seven, 46.2 per cent, had eighth-grade schooling or less. In other words, nearly half the rural ministers had no more than elementary educations. Twenty-one had some measure of high school training, but only three of these had completed the four years. Taking the four-county sample as indicative of general conditions, it is seen that 68.8 per cent, or nearly three-fourths, of rural ministers have less than high school educations.

Such limited academic training is of course a barrier to study in the more advanced phases of theological work. It also means that the minister can have little access to advanced recent knowledge dealing with even the practical phases of his work. It tends to isolate the minister from progressive developments in related fields and from the experience of successful ministers elsewhere.

This lack of academic training is becoming a source of

TABLE XIV

Formal Schooling of 80 Rural Ministers in Four Selected Counties

County	Grades Elementary								Grades High School				Years College				Degree	Years Seminary			Seminary Degrees
	1	2	3	4	5	6	7	8	9	10	11	12	1	2	3	4	A.B.	1	2	3	B.D.
Calhoun	1	1	4		2	2		3	4	4		2		3	1	1	5		1		1
Dallas			2	3	3	2	2	4	6	1	1		2	1	1		2				1
Mississippi								7	1	1		1		3							
Northumberland		1															3		1		4
All Counties	1	2	6	3	5	4	2	14	11	6	1	3	2	7	2	1	10		2		6

Note: Figures for elementary and high school represent grades completed. Figures for college and seminary represent years completed or in which now registered. All figures represent the whole amount of schooling of each individual, except the B.D.'s, which are also included among the A.B.'s.

embarrassment to the minister in his own parish. Rural education is steadily being extended and improved. High schools
for colored children are more numerous than they have been,
and high school graduates consequently are more numerous
even in the country church. For the minister to be beneath the
young of his parish in any important particular is obviously
a handicap. It is one of the factors responsible for the lack of
pastoral participation in young people's work (see Chapter
Seven). Certainly it jeopardizes the pastor's ability to lead his
young people effectively.

College Training

At the time this study was made, twelve of the eighty
ministers had received or were receiving some measure of
college instruction. Ten had completed four years of college
and held A.B. degrees. Five of these were in Calhoun County,
two in Dallas, and three in Northumberland. No rural minister in Mississippi County had been college trained.

Professional Training

Six ministers out of the eighty held Bachelor of Divinity
degrees, and two were still students in seminaries. That is to
say, only eight out of eighty ministers have or are receiving
professional preparation for their pastorates. If this study is
indicative of general Southern conditions, it means that only
10 per cent of the Negro rural ministry are professionally
prepared. It would seem that this is a most significant fact for
the character of rural religion. It jeopardizes the whole task of
propagating and transmitting Christianity in enlightened and
practicable forms.

Yet it is likely that ten per cent is a high estimate for the proportion of seminary trained men. Of the six ministers with Bachelor of Divinity degrees, four were in Northumberland County, Virginia. This state, however, is not in the deep South, where the bulk of the rural Negro population is to be found. If Calhoun County in South Carolina, Dallas County in Alabama, and Mississippi County in Arkansas be taken as more truly representative of the Southern states where Negroes are more numerous, it is seen that only two rural pastors out of seventy-three have had seminary training. This amounts to 2.8 per cent of the ministers serving rural charges.

Character of the Training

In Chapter Twelve something will be said of the character of the schools in which the ministers receive their training. When it is considered that many ministers are now elderly men and received their schooling years, even decades, ago, at a time when Southern educational facilities were not the equal of what they are today; and when it is considered further that few Southern schools or seminaries have first class or A ratings, the quality of the ministerial training as it was found is perhaps considerably lower than that suggested by the mention of grades.

In no case investigated was the professional training received of such nature as to prepare men specifically for the rural ministry. In every case it was the customary theological education, without courses in rural sociology, rural economics, and other phases of rural life. This lack of specialized training is not by any means peculiar to the Negro ministry. It is characteristic of American theological education in general. Only in very recent years has specific rural training been offered in any American seminary (see Chapter Twelve).

Knowledge of Rehabilitation Techniques

One of the essential elements in the rural minister's preparation is the ability to lead his people into the more abundant life—that is, to help them attain a standard of living that is more abundant economically and socially as well as spiritually.

To determine the pastor's ability along this line a series of leading questions was asked during interviews with sixty-five ministers, such as: "Do you know how to initiate cooperative projects for the purchase of food, feed, fertilizer, implements, or land?" "Do you know how to set up Federal savings and loan clubs?" "Do you cooperate with the state and Federal agencies working in your county?" On the basis of answers to these, along with the answers to other questions dealing with the social, moral, and economic conditions of his people, a judgement of the minister's knowledge of rehabilitation techniques was formed.

The knowledge of ten ministers was rated as good. That of sixteen others was rated as fair. Thirty-one ministers were rated as having definitely poor knowledge, and eight ministers appeared to have no knowledge of such techniques at all. That is, fifty-five out of sixty-five ministers had only fair or less knowledge about rehabilitating the people whom they serve, and more than half had little knowledge or none.

The implication of the figures is clear. The church, which is the chief agency in the rural South capable of helping the rural people, is in the hands of leadership poorly equipped to render this vital service. It is not implied here that the church as an institution should operate farms or keep cooperative stores, but it is implied that the pastor should be able to furnish the intellectual and spiritual inspiration as well as the practical information that would guide the people into undertaking these very necessary rehabilitation measures. There are cases, although still too few, in which pastors by giving devoted and informed leadership have been the means of transforming the life of needy communities.

Attitudes Toward Rural Work

An essential part of the minister's preparation for his work is his attitude toward it, that is, his reason for being in it and his intention to continue in it or leave it. Table XV indicates something of the attitudes of eighty-three ministers. Sixty-three, or about three-fourths, stated that they were in the rural pastorate through voluntary choice. The choice was based on (1) a desire to serve in a needy situation, and (2) a genuine preference for rural people and rural work. As a rule, both reasons were given together, but in a few cases one or the other was the sole ground for choosing the rural pastorate.

In three instances ministers stated that they were in the rural pastorate because they felt it was the Lord's will that they serve in this field, indicating that if they felt it were not his will, they would soon change fields. Their feeling was definitely a modification of a purely voluntary choice.

In discussing the choice of the rural field, some ministers pointed out what they considered to be advantages of rural work. Briefly summarized, these advantages were:

1. Rural people are more agreeable and easier to work with than city people.

2. A rural church does not require the constant intimate attention of the city church—the pastor has more time for himself and for other work.

3. Rural people are more generous in making provision for the pastor than city people.

TABLE XV

REASONS GIVEN BY 83 RURAL MINISTERS FOR
PASTORING RURAL CHARGES

COUNTY	CHOICE	ASSIGNMENT OR CALL FROM CONFERENCE	PLAN TO STAY
Calhoun	17	9	18
Dallas	32	6	30
Mississippi	7	5	6
Northumberland	7	0	6
All Counties	63	20	60

While some of these so-called advantages could be questioned from various points of view, particularly that of time devoted to causes other than the rural church, they do stand as the ground on which many of the men in the rural pastorate base their choice. One rural minister, yet in his early forties, had just refused a call to the second-largest church in the county seat, a city of seventy thousand, at a beginning salary of eighteen hundred dollars a year. His reasons were that he could make as much or more from his three rural churches in the course of a year, and he would have neither the constant work nor worry of a present-day city pastorate. Also, having more time to himself, he would be able to continue his academic and theological studies at a school in the county seat where he lived. At the time, he was taking second-year college work along with theological studies leading to the Bachelor of Theology degree.

Twenty rural pastors, or about one-fourth of the eighty-three, stated frankly that they were in the rural pastorate either because they had been assigned to it, or because it was a rural church that called them first and no city church as yet had done so.

In only two of these twenty instances were the pastors definitely dissatisfied with rural work as they encountered it. In the eighteen other cases, the ministers stated that rural pastoring was not objectionable in itself and that it had some attractive features about it. But they felt either that city work was better work or higher work, or they liked city life and preferred pastoring city churches.

Nearly three-fourths of the ministers stated that they planned to continue in the rural pastorate. Most of these said they looked upon their pastorates as a life work and had no desire to change.

Considerable difference was found in the age levels of the men who were in the rural pastorate by choice and those who were in it by call or assignment. Taking the age of forty-five as a division, it was found that 20.6 per cent of those voluntarily choosing were under forty-five years of age, while 45.0 per cent of those assigned were under forty-five. This indicates that more than twice as many young men enter the rural pastorate by assignment as enter it by choice. It probably means also that twice as many young men will leave the rural pastorate as soon as the first opportunity arises, thus depriving the most needy area of the most vigorous and active leadership.

The Rural Minister's Conception of His Role

Another of the factors determining ministerial effectiveness is the minister's conception of his role in the rural community, that is, what he feels he can do and ought to do for his people. Certainly this would determine the nature and extent of his program. The effort was made, therefore, to have each minister state as fully as possible what he conceived his place and duty as a rural minister to be.

Forty-eight, or more than half of the eighty-three ministers, stated that their primary duty was to preach. They felt that though a minister's tasks in a community are varied, and he is called on to do many things, yet his major function, his unique function in the community, is that of preaching the gospel. This was expressed in varied language. Some said "to preach," others "to save souls," one "to slay sin," but all indicated that they felt the primary responsibility of the minister was to preach the gospel in the community.

A smaller number of ministers stated that their main task was to help or serve the people. If this was to be achieved by preaching, then that should be their major aim. But if by a wider, more active program, then this would be stressed. They felt that their main task was to improve the life of their people, and to shape their ministry to attain this end.

Nearly all the ministers had two or more elements in their conceptions of their task. Even those who put preaching first also added "to teach," or "to help the folk," or "to better the community." Many said their duty was "to help the people spiritually and physically."

Where the expression "to teach" was used, it referred to

pastoral leadership by precept and example, rather than to systematic adult education. Yet, since so few of the ministers engage in any type of leadership other than verbal and are in their parishes for such little time, "to teach" meant in most cases to tell the people about their sins and their duties.

On the whole, the rural ministers gave evidence of a limited conception of their task as community leaders. While over half stated definitely that their major function was preaching, and the remainder made more inclusive statements, few had done anything to implement preaching with more concrete activities. It must be remembered too, as was shown above, that few rural ministers have adequate knowledge of activities other than preaching. Thus, with limited academic and professional training, and with poor knowledge of rehabilitation techniques, the conclusion is inescapable that many rural ministers can do little other than preach the gospel and "save souls."

The most striking description of his role was given by a minister in Calhoun County, who after a protracted period of difficult labor in an unresponsive church, stated that his conception of his role just now was to "get out from down there just as fast as I can."

Occupations Other Than Preaching

Most rural ministers engage in some kind of work other than service in their churches. The reasons for this appear to be: (1) Many rural ministers find it necessary to do outside work in order to have an adequate income. It has already been shown (Chapter Five) that few single rural churches can afford to employ a minister full time. Yet even where a minister has several churches, and from them all receives a respectable income, he still engages in some kind of employment besides preaching. It therefore seems (2) that it is the accepted custom for the rural pastor to engage in other than religious work. Certainly this is true for the rural ministry to a far greater extent than is customary for the city pastor. In most cases the rural parish is not an intensively pastored parish. As is shown elsewhere (Chapters Six, Seven, and Eleven) rural laymen carry on the work of the church with far less ministerial leadership than is the case with urban congregations. Since less time is devoted to pastoring, it is not only accepted, but it is almost expected that the rural minister will use his open time in some sort of lucrative employment.

The readiness with which the rural pastor's outside employment is accepted may work to the church's disadvantage. In the case of a rural church that has possibilities of being built up into a self-supporting full-time charge, this development is frequently missed because the minister has other interests besides the full development of his charge. In other words, outside pastoral employment is a cause as well as a result of the lack of pastoring in the rural community.

On the other hand, it may work to the church's advantage. The fact that a pastor can do various things to assure his support enables a church of limited means to get at least the partial services of a man they could not otherwise employ at all.

Table XVI shows the occupations besides preaching of eighty-one ministers who pastored rural churches. Seventeen, or approximately one-fifth, 21 per cent, had no other occupations whatever. Nine of these seventeen were elderly men who did not care to or were not able to do more than their pastorate required. Eight were pastors of three or more churches who said they had no time for other work.

TABLE XVI

PRINCIPAL OCCUPATIONS BESIDES PREACHING OF 81 RURAL MINISTERS IN FOUR SELECTED COUNTIES

COUNTY	NO OTHER OCCU-PATIONS	FARM-ING	PART-TIME FARM-ING	TEACH-ING	SKILLED TRADES	OTHER WORK	STU-DENT
Calhoun	2	8	4	3	3	4	3
Dallas	12	2	8	2	0	6	3
Mississippi	3	1	0	0	3	4	0
Northumberland	0	0	4	2	0	3	1
All Counties	17	11	16	7	6	17	7

Approximately three-fourths of the ministers, sixty-four, were engaged in other activity. Eleven were full-time farmers; sixteen were part-time farmers (that is, they farmed on a small scale); seven were teachers, of whom one was a college and seminary teacher, and three were high school principals; six worked as carpenters or in other trades; seventeen engaged in other types of work highly varied, such as: public stenographer, saw mill laborer, banker, barber and bootblack, common laborer, handy man in a store, real estate dealer, cosmetics salesman, porter, assistant rural mail carrier. Seven were students.

Summary

In considering the Negro rural minister's preparation for his work, a number of qualifying factors had to be taken into account. For example, it was necessary to recognize the distinction between formal schooling on the one hand and the practical acquirement of knowledge on the other. It was necessary to recognize, too, that knowledge acquired out of school could be quite as effective as that derived through schooling. Further, it was necessary to recognize the value of innate intelligence and leadership ability as compared with formal training. Frequently in this study it was found that a rural minister who was intelligent and possessed the ability to work with people and to lead them was a more attractive, though not more efficient, rural leader than a formally trained man who lacked these abilities. Thus, one bishop of a Negro denomination whose episcopal district is largely rural said that, while he did not discount the value of schooling, he preferred "any day" an untrained man of ability to a trained man who lacked it. Virtually the same opinion was expressed by other church leaders.

But recognizing the value of informal learning and innate ability does not at all disparage formal training. In only two cases in this study were men of lesser training found who had in any way exceeded the better trained men around them. Even these two complained that they could have done much more if they had had better training.

In general, it was found that untrained men had definite limitations:

1. They confined themselves to a preaching ministry and to the raising of funds. Their preaching, while popular because of the preacher's gifts, lacked the sounder values of truly constructive leadership, and such funds as were raised were generally loosely accounted for and unwisely spent (see Chapter Five).

2. Untrained men appeared to be less concerned about the material welfare of their people; they appeared less willing and less able to undertake efforts to improve living conditions.

3. Untrained men appeared to be less aware of the moral, social, and economic problems of their people. They knew little of methods of discovering the problems, and less of ways of dealing with them. For example, in no case had an untrained minister made a parish or community survey (see Chapter Nine).

4. The achievements of the untrained tended to center in one or two specialities, such as a crusade against dancing, or in one case, a campaign to improve houses. They seldom attained the rounded ministry.

5. As a rule, it was the untrained minister who experienced greatest embarrassment in the work with young people (Chapter Seven), and who found the task of leading them most difficult.

In contrast to the limitations of the untrained, the highest examples of effective rural ministry found in this study were all the work of the most highly trained men (see Chapter Twelve).

In short, although there is quite a tendency in rural areas to extol the virtues of the untrained minister, there is no justification for it. Training without ability is naturally ineffective, but ability without training is limited also. The ideal, of course, is the able man well trained. But of the two, schooling is the more essential, and is especially important for the minister of average capacities.

With nearly half the ministers possessing only grade-school training, that is, education equal to that of a twelve-year-old child, or less; and with almost three-fourths of them possessing less than high school training, that is, education equal to that of a sixteen-year-old youth, or less, it is easy to see the handicap under which the present rural ministry labors, and to appreciate the difficulties such a handicap can cause.

Those who aspire to lead can ill afford to be behind those to be led in any essential particular. Improvement in education of the rural minister is a cause for immediate action both by the individual minister and by the national body to which he belongs.

In addition to academic training there is need for professional training in dealing with problems of rural folk. Conceding that the minister's chief function is to preach, if the preaching is not related to problems of daily life it is preaching "in the air." It may be quite popular and powerful, and may lift its hearers to great emotional heights; but when the service is over, it leaves them to descend into the same problems they left before going to church. It is the persistent problems of daily life that make Christian living difficult. In other words, along with constructive preaching there must go a program of effective life improvement. Both are dependent upon training.

Chapter Nine

THE CHURCH AND SOCIAL PROBLEMS

General Southern Rural Conditions

In general, the level on which the Negro lives in the South is not only below the American standard, but it is also below the standard of whites in his same social and cultural class in the South. For example, the average value of farms owned by Negroes is less than that for whites; the lot of the Negro tenant is in many ways worse than that of the white; the Negro's income for farm and non-farm labor in the South is less than that for whites; the general condition of Negro housing in the rural South is worse than that for whites; community services available to Negroes such as transportation, telephone, telegraph, schooling, and recreation, are poorer than the same services available to whites; expenditures of Negro families for food, clothing, and medical care are lower than those of whites. In short, while all of the elements listed here are lower than the national average for the whites of the rural South, they are even lower still for the Negroes. This means that the Negro's level of living in the rural South is perhaps the lowest in the nation.[1]

[1] See Chapter Two.

The Church and Social Problems

When we turn to consider the work of the church in these social problems, a striking correlation at once comes to view: where living conditions are highest, church life is best; where living conditions are lowest, church life is poorest.[1] For example, in Northumberland County, where farm ownership is highest and family income greatest, the largest proportion of educated, resident ministers is to be found. In Mississippi County, where tenancy is highest and income lowest, the smallest proportion of resident pastors is found, and the preparation of the pastors in the county is lowest. This makes inescapable the conclusion that in quality of service to its people, the rural church follows advantages (favored living conditions) instead of seeking to increase advantages for those who do not have them. It also means that quality of church life rises as living standards of the people rise. Therefore, it is imperative that the church improve life among its people, for as the people improve, so does the church.

Pastoral Awareness of Problems

The best way in which a minister can become accurately aware of the conditions and problems of his people is through a careful community survey. This is really the *sine qua non* of effective pastoral service. Yet in only three cases had the pastors of 108 rural churches selected for study surveyed their communities, and these three were all in Northumberland County.

[1] By "church life" is meant both the worshipful activities of the church member and the services the church renders its community.

One of the three surveys had been made very carefully by the pastor with the aid of persons in the church. The other two had not been done quite as carefully, but they did afford the pastors fairly accurate information about their parishes. All of the three pastors making the surveys had had some college training, and two held Bachelor of Divinity degrees.

In a few other cases the pastors appeared to have a fairly accurate working knowledge of their people and their problems. This was true of one minister in Calhoun County, two in Dallas, and one in Mississippi County. In each case they had gained their knowledge by frequent, systematic pastoral visits, and by devoting time and thought to parish needs. In only one of these cases, the one found in Mississippi County, was the minister uneducated. Of the remaining three, one minister was a teacher in a seminary and the other two were high school graduates.

There is a definite correlation between education and the first step to good pastoring—that is, an accurate knowledge on the part of the minister about the membership of his church. To be sure, not every educated minister in this study had made a survey or knew his people accurately, but with one exception it was only the educated ones who had. In short, it is evident that training is essential to effective work in the parish field. While some ministers had achieved a fair working knowledge of their fields without making surveys, there were many phases of personal and community life about which they were not definite. Above all, they did not have the one thing the rural Negro church so badly needs, and that is *records* upon which personal and community development can be followed through.

Home Ownership

In most cases the pastors were only generally aware of home ownership and housing conditions of their people. In only seven cases out of 108 could pastors state definitely the number of their members who owned their homes. In other cases they could only reply that "a few," or "some," or "a good many" owned homes. They were dependent entirely on general impressions and had no other basis for their statements. Only in a few plantation sections where all of the members were renters could the pastors answer accurately that none were home owners. This lack of interest in determining the number who owned homes would seem to indicate a lack of interest in the whole matter of home ownership.

Housing Conditions

In considering the relation between the church and rural housing, a number of qualities were stipulated in determining what was meant by a good home. Chief among them were: (1) state of repair, (2) sufficiency of rooms, (3) availability of water, (4) sanitary facilities—screens and toilets, and (5) beautification—paint and flowers.

Only three pastors out of 106 had detailed, accurate information on housing conditions among their members. The rest were able to give only general impressions. The pastors of twenty-five churches described the housing of their people as good, sixty as fair, seventeen as poor, and four as bad. Very often the answer "fair" meant fair according to the prevailing standards in that vicinity. This would reduce "fair" to "poor" in many instances. Thus, a fair house for a sharecropper is a poor house by most standards. Consequently, a large proportion of the homes rated fair could be classed as poor or even bad.

The significant point is that with the homes of sixty parishes, 56.6 per cent, being classed as only fair, and twenty-one, 19.8 per cent, as poor or bad, the pastors of three-fourths of the 106 churches are generally aware that housing conditions among their people are unsatisfactory. But only three had gone as far as making a study from which they could determine how many homes needed improving, what each needed, and how the dwellers could be helped in the task of improvement.

The chief reason given by the pastors for the poor condition of homes was the refusal of landlords to make necessary repairs or improvements. This reason was given by the pastors of sixty-one out of eighty-three churches, 73.5 per cent. A much smaller number, ten, cited indifference on the part of the dweller as largely responsible for conditions, and twelve cited the poverty of the persons occupying the premises.

Undoubtedly the fact that landlords make only the most necessary repairs and few if any improvements is responsible for much bad rural housing in the South. It does not account, however, for the poor condition of many privately owned homes. Nor does it obscure the fact that there is much a tenant can do to make his dwelling livable and attractive if he is minded to do so.

Further, the lack of repair is not wholly responsible for the uncleanliness of many rural homes, which is also a part of poor conditions. One minister in Mississippi County who had done much to improve the homes in his parish, when asked about the condition of homes, asked in reply; "Do you mean the outside of the house or the inside?" He was aware of the share the tenant can play in bettering living conditions even under the handicaps of tenant status.

In his work with his people, this minister had achieved a considerable amount of home improvement in the parish. He first preached about better homes, but getting little response, he began to beautify the dilapidated parsonage, enlisting the help of the people in the work. From improving the minister's home they gained the incentive to improve their own. Today the homes of that parish are much better than when the minister came. He has demonstrated clearly that in spite of poverty and other handicaps, there is much the country Christian can do to improve his life in the South, given proper leadership. Perhaps more than any other institution the church can supply this necessary leadership in home improvement.

Methods of Pastoral Aid

Seeing the condition, what is the ministry's way of meeting it?

The pastors of all the 106 churches speak about the condition in their sermons. Considering, however, the general nature of rural preaching and the infrequency of it (see Chapter Six), the effectiveness of preaching alone as an incentive to improvement can well be questioned.

In more practical and intimate leadership the record is not as good. In Northumberland County five churches have home improvement clubs and garden clubs. Outside of that county no other church was found that had such an activity, except that of the pastor in Mississippi County who by the example of beautifying the parsonage had achieved a large measure of home improvement.

Sixteen ministers stated that they mention home improvement in their pastoral visits. But with the limited amount of such visiting, the efficacy of this method is also almost nil. To interest people in a way of living different from that which now obtains requires leadership of much greater constancy than can be achieved from an occasional word of advice.

Lacking home clubs and other effective means of improvement, it would seem that rural ministers would at least give every cooperation to county agents, home demonstration agents, health officers, and other workers, whose specific task in rural areas is to achieve higher standards of life. Yet out of the pastors of 106 churches, only nine stated that they actively cooperate with rural workers. Practically all give incidental assistance, but they do not link their churches in any definite or organized way to the rural extension program.

Two county agents and three home demonstration agents working in the counties studied were asked to what extent rural ministers cooperate with them in their work. They uniformly replied that the great majority of the pastors give no active cooperation. They seldom encounter real antagonism, but they do encounter what is almost as bad, indifference, ineffectiveness, and many worthless promises.

Each agent said that in his county there are a few ministers who appreciate extension work, and make it an integral part of the church program. They give the extension worker excellent, active co-operation. But these are rare exceptions. Most ministers are indifferent, and give only incidental support.

One county agent, an active, influential man in his county,

said that he approaches most rural ministers simply as a token of respect to the pastoral office, and to escape their open opposition. As for getting cooperation in his work, he has learned to depend on the people rather than on their pastors. He also said that county authorities and leaders of civic movements such as the War Bond drives, health drives, and community improvement efforts, were coming to realize the uncooperativeness of the ministry, and were depending upon it less and less for leadership in significant popular efforts.

The agents attributed pastoral ineffectiveness to the absentee pastorate as much as to lack of training or personal failings.

Economic Betterment

Basic to all economic welfare is the matter of income. If income is low, level of living is low, and progress of any kind becomes proportionately harder. Yet there are two elements in the matter of income, both of which are determinative of how the earner lives and how he can improve his standard of living. One is the amount that the worker earns, the second is what he does with what he earns—the extent to which he uses his earnings advantageously and wisely.

It is granted that there is little the Negro rural minister can do directly to influence rates of pay in the agricultural South. These are based upon regional, national, and international agricultural, commercial, and industrial conditions that are far beyond his poor power to alter. Also in the case of the Negro agricultural worker the low rates may be due to a racial differential that the minister likewise is unable to alter as he would like.

But there are ways in which the Negro rural minister can

serve the economic welfare of his people. It is generally known that the Negro tenant, especially the sharecropper, suffers not only from low pay, but also from dishonest settlement. In many cases he does not get and he dares not demand the little income that he has earned. This dishonest dealing is not a matter of world market conditions. It is a matter of personal morals and personal relationships, and it is a field in which the minister can well serve. More than any other leader, the minister has the opportunity to be a good-will ambassador in securing fairer settlements for his folk. There are cases in which country pastors have served with heroic wisdom and courage to improve both individual and group relationships between landlord and tenant. But such cases are few. The rural ministers as a whole have not yet come to regard representation of their people in difficult personal situations as a definite part of the ministerial office.

There are other things the minister can do to help his people economically. The establishment of a cooperative credit union in a community would do much to eliminate the disastrous, usurious rates the rural Negro must often pay for financial assistance. Cooperative buying of feed, fertilizer, implements, and other necessities would help the people to get greatest value from the little that they earn.

Such things are being done, but in all too many cases the ministry plays no part. In Dallas County, for example, it was found that four farmers in a colored community had pooled their savings in first payment on a tract of land that none of them could have purchased individually. They work the land together, and after payments are made, divide profits equally. The land, an exhausted plantation, was sold at extortionate rates, and the county agent is not optimistic in his feeling as to the purchasers' ability to pay out. The effort represents, however, a significant attempt at voluntary cooperation, but so far it has enjoyed no ministerial assistance.

In another Dallas County community, two burial societies had joined their funds and had purchased several hundred acres that they were selling in small plots to their members at low rates of interest. This project seems to have good promise of success, but this, too, is wholly without benefit of clergy.

The conviction that ministers can be effective in bettering the economic condition of their people is based upon the observation that some rural ministers have done so. For example, in Northumberland County one minister was able to count thirty-one farm homesteads that over a period of seven years had been bought by young couples in his church under his suggestion and guidance. Also, at the time of this study, he was organizing several farmers in his church into a cooperative club for the purchase of several expensive, modern farm machines that none of them could buy alone.

Another pastor in the same county, through the church's alumni clubs,[1] visits his members who are working in industrial centers, and helps them in the wise investment of their earnings, particularly in the purchase of farms in their home county. The worth of this for the post-war period of economic readjustment is obvious.

Needless to say the two ministers mentioned here were trained, they lived with their people, and they were dedicated to the rural ministry as a worthy, life-long vocation.

[1] See Chapter Four.

The Pastor and Rural Morals

The opinions of the pastors of 102 rural churches regarding moral conditions in their parishes was predominantly favorable. The pastors of sixty-nine churches reported that general moral conditions in their parishes were good, twenty-two reported they were fair, and only seven, or 6.9 per cent, reported them as definitely bad to the point that they constituted a pastoral problem. Four ministers had no definite opinions on the subject.

In considering the judgments of the pastors regarding moral conditions in their parishes, several qualifications should be kept in mind:

1. Except for the three cases in Northumberland County, no minister had made a detailed study of his community. This means that the judgment on moral conditions was much like that on economic conditions—a general impression.

2. The preponderance of favorable opinion could mean: (a) that moral conditions among Christians in the country are higher than among non-Christians. There is some reason to believe that this is the case. Since in the country personal behavior is more evident, those professing Christianity feel impelled to live up to it. Or (b) it could mean that ministers do not know their communities well.

The general impression gained in making this study was that moral life among the rural church members was very much as the ministers described it. This impression came from living in some of the communities, as well as from conversations with many laymen and ministers.

It was found that in sixteen parishes there is a great deal of liquor drinking, according to the pastors, and in seven parishes moral conditions are bad. Five of these were plantation sections in which the landlords protected gambling, drinking, and other forms of vice. One extension worker stated that there are two kinds of places landlords support: the church and the road house. Both hold men on the plantation, but men of different types. His observation was found to be true on some of the large, highly capitalized plantations in his county, but not on all plantations and not in all counties.

In the problem communities, the ministers cited as the chief moral evils:

> whiskey
> sexual immorality
> illegal or common law cohabitation
> gambling
> road houses

One minister attributed the sexual looseness in his community to the large number of men taken from their homes by the war. Another attributed it to movies. As to the number of broken homes in their parishes, lacking an accurate count, seventeen answered "a few," seventeen answered "none," and one said there were "many." According to the ministers most of the homes were broken by the deaths of the husbands. In the case of one minister who had made a survey, his parish contained a little settlement of widows whose husbands had all been lost at sea while working on fishing vessels. At the time of this study he was performing a second wedding ceremony for one of these widows, and was quite happy about it. It was the impression of the minister that far fewer homes were broken by divorce and desertion than by death.

Pastoral Effectiveness

The rural pastor's chief instrument for working with moral problems is of course his sermon. But its limitations in this case, as in the case of economic problems, was its lack of concrete constructive suggestion, which normally is the result of training; and its infrequency, which greatly weakens its effect. Because most pastors lived away from their parishes they were not able to give their people the intimate guidance upon which moral improvement depends.

In only three churches out of 106 did the pastors indicate that they were in any way restrained in speaking about moral conditions. All others said they were quite free to speak about morals at any time.

Chapter Ten

RACE RELATIONS

In summary terms, the race problem may be described as the effort of a dominant majority group to inflict prejudicial, discriminative, suppressive treatment upon a disadvantaged minority group in every area of life, economic, social, civic, and religious; and as the effort of the minority group to escape this treatment and rise above the suppressed condition. In the presence of the American democratic ideal this treatment of a minority element is unreasonable and immoral. In the light of the Christian religion it is unrighteous. It is this conflict between ideals and practices, between the desire for fairness on the one hand and the tendency to mistreat on the other, that turns the Negro's presence in America into the "Negro problem." The conflict has recently led one great scholar to describe it as "An American Dilemma."[1]

The problem has a long history that goes back to the earliest days of Negro slavery. At the present time it is a complex of fears and feelings, attitudes and actions, taboos and liberties,

[1] *An American Dilemma,* by Gunnar Myrdal, Vol. I, pp. xli-li. New York, Harper and Brothers, 1944.

heroic protestations and fast-fixed social customs, efforts at kindness and deliberate mistreatment, high philanthropy and base meanness, all existing in disturbing confusion in the presence of modern ideals and conditions. The whole is involved in an emotional heat that makes clear thought and direct action most difficult.

The race problem is one factor that is responsible for the disparate position of the Negro in contemporary American economy. It is a cause of low income, poor housing, unequal education, disfranchisement, inequality before the law, segregated, unequal public accommodations and privileges, and incidentally, of the separate Negro church. It leads to the thinking that seeks to justify these practices, and to the protests that aim to correct them.

In the midst of this tangle of thoughts and motives, the rural Negro church seeks to find its way to the more abundant life. This chapter attempts to estimate the part this church is playing in solving the persistent problem.

Ministerial Attitudes

During the study of the church in its relation to the race problem, pastors of 105 churches were interviewed at some length. The ministers were surprisingly optimistic in their statements about the problem. In the great majority of the church communities, eighty-three, or 79 per cent, race relations were described as good. In a much smaller number, 21, or 20 per cent, relations were described as fair. Only one minister indicated that relations in his community were bad. Yet three counties of this study, Calhoun, Dallas, and Mississippi, are located in the lower South. They are counties in which the plantation system still prevails, where the Negro population is large, and tensions and repressive measures generally are severe. It is a commonly accepted fact that the problem is worst where the number of Negroes is largest.

TABLE XVII

OPINIONS OF PASTORS OF 105 RURAL CHURCHES ON THE
PRESENT STATUS OF RACE RELATIONS IN THEIR
CHURCH COMMUNITIES

COUNTY	GOOD	FAIR	BAD	TOTAL
Calhoun	28	3	0	31
Dallas	39	6	0	45
Mississippi	7	12	1	20
Northumberland	9	0	0	9
All Counties	83	21	1	105
	79%	20%	0.1%	100%

The fact that so many ministers describe as good conditions that by almost any standard of measurement are bad necessitates considerable explanation. (1) The term "good" as used by ministers is a comparative term. It means good as compared with former times or other places. As one minister expressed it, "They may not be too good now, but they have been worse." (2) It also means lack of recent violence or cases of severe mistreatment. Every minister said that there had been no recent racial clashes in his community. In some sections of the Lower South this is definitely good. (3) The statements indicate acceptance of the status quo in race relations, but do not indicate satisfaction with it. Many ministers qualified the term "good" by adding "good for this section," or just "good considering." This shows that they know conditions are not what they should be. (4) The statements indicate the pacific tendency of most ministers. Many were quite dissatisfied with conditions, but they prefer not to change if change involves violence or bloodshed or serious trouble. They are given to the good-will method of improvement, and are inclined to identify quiet with good. Thus, again, they will suffer present conditions and think of them as good, especially as compared with the trouble that attempted change may bring. (5) The term "good" probably indicates professional optimism. The ministers know the lot of their people is hard. They also know that a hopeful, optimistic attitude is essential to both survival and progress. They therefore talk optimistically when there is little present ground for it; they say conditions are good when in reality they are bad.

All ministers reported that there had been no recent clashes between groups in their communities. Their statements did not include cases of individual mistreatment, such as police brutality, for many of these cases were heard about as the study was made. They referred only to group conflicts, such as riots. It was on the absence of such clashes that ministers based their opinions that conditions were good.

Progress in Race Relations

As to whether or not relations between the races are improving, the ministers were equally optimistic. In seventy-two out of ninety-eight church communities, or 73.5 per cent, relations were depicted as definitely getting better. In about one-tenth as many, seven, they were regarded as no better than they had been. In nineteen communities, 19.4 per cent of the total, the pastors were uncertain as to any improvement in relations. Not a single minister felt that relations were getting worse.

Allowing for professional optimism and other qualifying factors mentioned above, the belief indicated by more than two-thirds of the ministers that relations between the races are improving is significant for several reasons. If their judgment is sound, improvement in race relations should tend to reduce precipitate, unplanned migration. One of the factors responsible for migration is the race problem in the South.

TABLE XVIII

OPINIONS OF PASTORS OF 98 RURAL CHURCHES ON IMPROVEMENT IN RACE RELATIONS IN THEIR CHURCH COMMUNITIES

COUNTY	RELATIONS GETTING BETTER	GETTING NO BETTER	UNCERTAIN	GETTING WORSE	TOTAL
Calhoun	22	0	8	0	30
Dallas	30	1	10	0	41
Mississippi	11	6	1	0	18
Northumberland	9	0	0	0	9
All Counties	72	7	19	0	98
	73.5%	7.1%	19.4%	0.0%	100%

Similarly, improvement should mean increased possibility of the Negro's developing a wholesome rural life in the South. The race problem is one, if not the major, barrier to the progress of the Negro farmer in the South.

When asked the basis for their opinion that relations between the races are improving, ministers in sixty-three cases gave as the primary evidence "no recent trouble," by which they meant no recent major outburst of violence, or cases of severe interracial tension. In fifty-one cases ministers based their opinions on the fact that whites were more cordial and more cooperative. One minister said that for the first time in his life he was seeing whites and Negroes working together without friction.

As to the causes of the improvement, the ministers cited the following:

The recent World War, requiring cooperation in the effort to win.

The ideals for which we fought the war.

Education.

The church and Christianity.

The present world trouble.

Negro protestation and agitation.

The New Deal.

The necessity of keeping Negro labor in the South, especially on the cotton plantations.

One minister stated that the cause of improvement in race relations in his community was the death of a landlord who had caused much trouble, and the coming of a new one who was much more understanding and cooperative.

A minister who felt that conditions were no better stated that while the effort to win the war had led to increased cooperation in some areas, in others it had created greater tension and bitterness that more than offset any advantages. He felt that the necessity of working together under compulsion was not good, and would breed future trouble.

In considering the statements of the ministers on the race problem, it must be remembered that their opinions were based on general impressions rather than on objective studies of conditions and relations. As has been said previously (Chapter Nine), only three ministers in this study had made community surveys. Most do not live in their parishes, and are in them only for short times (Chapter Six). While their impressions may be quite accurate and dependable, they are impressions, and possess all the limitations of impressions.

Christian Cooperation

In this chapter the question of race relations is being considered from the point of view of the rural Negro minister. As a member of the disadvantaged minority group, he is not able by his own power alone to do much to affect relationships with the majority group, or to change conditions as they exist between the two groups. He must have some measure of cooperation from the majority element if he is to be effective in the area of race relations. Seeing the matter from the church's position, cooperation between the white and colored Christian forces is necessary if the church is to play an effective part in solving the Southern rural race problem.

Cooperation with White Laymen

It was the opinion of seventy-four out of seventy-nine ministers, 93.7 per cent, that white laymen were friendly and cooperative toward the Negro church. In nearly every case the ministers cited financial contributions to the colored church as evidence and as the principal form of white cooperation. While this was the main form of cooperation, there were a few others. Six ministers reported that whites visited their churches frequently, and three reported an exchange of visits between choirs and young people's groups. Two of these three cases were in Mississippi County; the other was in Calhoun.

One minister reported that in the effort to beautify his church, white workers, who themselves were churchmen, assisted voluntarily in painting the interior of the church. Such cases, however, are very few. Most whites cooperate with the Negro church by giving a small sum of money when approached. And it should be added that their cooperation is seldom sought in any other way.

TABLE XIX

OPINIONS OF PASTORS OF 79 RURAL CHURCHES ON COOPERATIVE ATTITUDE OF WHITE LAYMEN IN THEIR CHURCH COMMUNITIES

COUNTY	COOPERATIVE	NOT COOPERATIVE	TOTAL
Calhoun	27	4	31
Dallas	25	0	25
Mississippi	14	1	15
Northumberland	8	0	8
All Counties	74	5	79
	93.7%	6.3%	100%

In the opinions of the ministers, the motives for the cooperation vary. (1) Business men frequently give to the colored church as a good will gesture, or as an advertisement. (2) Many white laymen regard the Negro church as a quieting influence in the community, an instrument that can keep down racial trouble, and they support it for this reason. (3) Many give to the colored church and share in its activities out of a purely Christian missionary motive, the same motive that leads, for example, to the establishment and support of home and foreign missions. Some of the cases cited above, such as that of the white workmen painting the colored church, are evidence of a spirit of Christian brotherhood at work.

Other than financial contributions and an occasional visit, there were few cases of cooperation of any kind found. This is not surprising, since the program of the rural church is so meager, and the pastor who could serve best as leader in promoting cooperative undertakings is seldom on the scene to give the necessary leadership.

Five ministers out of seventy-nine reported that the whites in their communities were not cooperative, but three of these added that they had made no effort to elicit such cooperation.

A further test on attitudes of whites was attempted by asking the ministers if they encountered opposition to their activities, such as to their preachments, or their program of community betterment. Out of seventy-six ministers replying, every one stated that no opposition was encountered. This unanimity could mean:

1. That the ministers are careful not to say or do things that will arouse the resentment and opposition of the whites.

2. The whites no longer regard the rural Negro church as a potential source of rebellion and trouble, and hence do not watch it so closely.

3. Or it could mean that the necessity for regulating thought and suppressing progressive ideas is passing with the plantation system and the growth of liberalism in the South.

Cooperation with White Ministers

The cooperation of the white ministers with the colored pastor and his church is not nearly as great as that of the white laymen. Out of seventy-five Negro ministers, only twenty indicated any measure of ministerial cooperation. Fifty-five, or 73.3 per cent, said they have little if any contact with their white colleagues.

TABLE XX

REPLIES OF PASTORS OF 75 RURAL CHURCHES IN RESPONSE TO THE QUESTION: "DO YOU HAVE ANY CONTACT WITH THE WHITE MINISTERS OF YOUR CHURCH COMMUNITY?"

COUNTY	"YES"	"NO"	TOTAL
Calhoun	6	23	29
Dallas	1	24	25
Mississippi	9	3	12
Northumberland	4	5	9
All Counties	20	55	75
	26.7%	73.3%	100%

One reason for the lack of contact is that in many Southern rural communities no white church is near the colored settlement. This is especially true, for example, of Dallas and Calhoun counties. In these counties the rural Negro population outnumbers the white, and many communities are wholly populated by Negroes or nearly so. Moreover, in these counties many whites own farms but live in the nearby towns. Often those who live in the open country go to church in the town. Thus, no white church was found in twenty-four Dallas County communities.

The second reason for the lack of interracial ministerial contact is that the white rural pastor, like the colored, is often an absentee pastor. Spending little time in their parishes save on meeting Sundays, the colored and white pastors have little chance to meet. Frequently they do not know each other's names. In seven cases the colored ministers had never seen the pastors of the white churches in their communities.

These two reasons account for most of the lack of co-operation, but there were a few cases where white and colored pastors lived in the same community and still had nothing to do with each other. One Negro minister reported that a white pastor refused to speak to him on the streets, although they had previously met. In two other cases colored ministers stated that the white pastors would have nothing to do with them personally, and would permit no measure of inter-church cooperation. The two most probable reasons for such unchristian behavior on the part of white pastors are (1) personal prejudice against Negroes, or (2) fear of the penalties even the white minister must pay in some Southern communi-ties if his association with a Negro of any profession is more intimate and more nearly on a basis of equality than the com-munity thinks it should be.

In one case a colored minister stated that he had no co-operation with the white minister because he had not sought it, did not want it, and did not plan to seek any cooperation in the future. He said: "I don't like them, I don't trust them, and I has as less to do with them as I possibly can." This was the only instance of such an attitude. The other Negro min-isters showed a desire for cooperation.

Twenty ministers reported cooperation. The activities men-tioned as evidence of cooperation were:

White ministers preach in colored churches—eight cases.
Colored ministers preach in white churches—three cases.
White and colored ministers conduct a joint revival—one case.

White ministers instruct and lend books to colored ministers
—seven cases.

White ministers active in interracial committees—one case.

It was found that the highest measure of ministerial cooperation was in Mississippi County. Two of the three instances in which Negro pastors were invited to preach in
white churches were in this county. The other was in Calhoun County. The one case in which a white and colored
pastor conducted a joint revival, preaching some nights in the
white church and some in the colored, with white and colored
members attending both churches, was in Mississippi County.
Yet this is a county in which most of the farmers, white and
colored, are sharecroppers. It is also the one with lowest
educational standards among the ministers (see Chapter
Eight) and in other respects the poorest type of church life.
It is surprising that in this county, where churches are poorest,
cooperation between ministers is greatest.

Effectiveness of White Ministers in Race Problems

The race problem in the rural South is explosive. Incidents
of the most trivial nature may lead to outbursts of most
serious violence; prejudices on the part of a person or a group
may lead to acts of brutal mistreatments of persons or groups.

In such moments the greatest need is men who can stand
for right, allay fears, disseminate understandings, insist upon
fair enforcement of laws, and who have the courage to work
to afford some measure of protection to the weaker, more
defenseless side. It would seem that here in these moments
of crisis are prime opportunities for white and colored ministers to serve in a most important way. The white minister's

chance for service is greater, since he represents the dominant, more empowered group. Yet it is the finding of this study that in moments of crisis in race relations, the white ministry generally is ineffective.

Thirty-four Negro rural ministers were interviewed who had had some experience with their white colleagues in cases of race trouble. Twelve said white ministers were effective in time of trouble, twenty-two said they were not.

Most of those giving negative answers felt that white ministers could do much to allay troubles if they would. One Negro minister said the white pastor in his community "would not touch" the problem under any circumstances, and another white pastor did not care to be bothered with it.

Of the twelve ministers who stated whites are effective, one said that the white minister in his community would support a person if the person were in the right. Another said that the white minister had stood for fair treatment in several instances of race friction.

The behavior of the white minister in time of crisis must not be confused with the general attitude of whites toward the racial problem, nor with his more normal efforts to improve race relations. It is very likely that most white ministers have a sense of Christian brotherhood, and would welcome more cooperation with their colored confrères if they were free to offer it. Also, many are willing to take some steps toward the attainment of better relations. This is indicated by the growing observance of Interracial Brotherhood Sunday in rural white Southern churches.[1]

[1] This statement is based on information from the Department of Race Relations of the Federal Council of Churches of Christ in America.

The Effectiveness of the Negro Minister in Improving Race Relations

Strikingly enough, the Negro ministry is not much more active than the white in making a direct attack on the disturbing race problem in the rural South. In order to get some idea of Negro ministerial activity in race relations, the general question was asked: "Are you able to do much to improve race relations in your church community?" The question was worded in this indefinite manner in order to serve as an opening to discussion in which the minister could describe any activities or achievement in his experience. Twenty-five ministers out of fifty-two gave affirmative answers, that is, indicated that they are doing something. A slightly larger number, twenty-seven, gave negative answers, indicating that they are doing nothing at all. In other words, more than half of the Negro ministers interviewed are doing little or nothing to improve race relations.

The chief reason for the inactivity is of course the absentee pastorate. Ministers are not in their parishes long enough to give their people leadership in this most pressing problem. This reason was given by all of the negative respondents. But what is more disturbing, sixteen of the inactive ministers stated that they did not regard race relations as within their field of responsibility. When asked how they could overlook such a vast and troublesome area in the life of their people, the most common reply was: "My job is to preach the gospel." Another common statement was that the race problem exists because the gospel is not preached enough. This last statement, of course, begs the question. It does not explain how a gospel preached in a separated church to the victimized side can affect the other side who never hear the preaching.

The ministers who said that they had worked to improve race relations gave the following as their activities:

Speaking to civil authorities about conditions.

Speaking to leading white citizens about conditions.

Interpreting tenants to landlords.

Advising Negroes on how to behave, especially returning soldiers.

At first view the statement, "advising Negroes on how to behave," may seem to indicate the minister's acceptance of subordinate status, and the effort to bring others into similar acceptance. This is due to the limited choice of words by the uneducated pastors. It was revealed in the interviews that what the ministers really were trying to do was to caution their people on the necessity of behaving so as to avoid violence. The rural ministry's pacific tendency has already been mentioned. Also, the avoidance of trouble in some rural situations may be at least temporarily wise and practical.

Summary

The race problem as it exists in the rural South is immoral and unchristian. It is an open challenge to rural Christian forces that neither the white church nor the colored church can avoid. The white church cannot justifiably ignore it, the Negro church cannot afford to. Betterment in race relations as they exist in the rural South today is an imperative as far as the church is concerned.

Yet in working for betterment neither church is as effective as it ought to be. To a limited degree white laymen cooperate with the Negro churches in their communities, but except in a relatively few cases, the cooperation consists mainly in making small financial donations upon request. There is little cooperation in church activities, and there are no projects for church or community improvement on which the white and colored church groups work together with equal interest and equal dignity as fellow Christians.

Because of the absentee pastorate, and also because of personal attitudes and fear, there is little cooperation between white and colored ministers as religious leaders of a community. In cases of race conflict, white ministers are not generally towers of strength standing for justice and peace, nor are they spokesmen for the weak. However, the general attitude of white ministers toward the racial situation and their efforts at improvement appear to be growing in fairness and courage.

Negro ministers are not nearly as effective as they ought to be or can be in a problem that so deeply determines the life and progress of their people. The absentee pastorate is partly responsible, but there is a lack of interest and an irresponsibility that are definite pastoral deficiencies.

While this study depicts the general prevailing conditions, it must not be overlooked that there are striking exceptions. For instance, in Northumberland County one colored minister had served as president of the local branch of the National Association for the Advancement of Colored People, had led the effort to attain better pay for colored school teachers, was highly respected in the community, and was one of the most influential persons in the county in working to improve or adjust relations between the races. Also, in a small South

Carolina town (outside the county of this study) the white ministerial association invited the colored ministers to meet with them periodically, to report cases of injustice or race friction, as well as to point out opportunities for improving conditions among the colored people of the community. The white and colored ministers, acting as a unit, would then undertake to correct wrongs and to better conditions. It must be repeated, however, that these cases, encouraging as they are, are the exceptions. They are not yet the general rule in the rural South.

Chapter Eleven

MINISTERIAL INFLUENCE IN
THE COMMUNITY

In the course of this study the attempt was made to determine the nature as well as the extent of pastoral influence in the rural community. To this end a number of laymen were interviewed and asked a series of leading questions. In some cases they were church leaders, such as deacons, stewards, stewardesses, church clerks, or Sunday school superintendents. But in about half the cases they were ordinary members who held no prominent positions in either church or community, and who therefore would be less likely to be strongly biased for or against the pastor.

Pastoral Visiting

When asked how many days per month the pastor visited in the parish, nearly half, 43.3 per cent, gave such answers as "a few," "once in a while," "seldom," or "very few." About one-third, 35.0 per cent, stated that their pastors visited only "on call," or "when needed." If these two sets of replies are added, it is seen that more than three-fourths of the laymen,

78.3 per cent, were aware that their pastors did not spend much time in their parishes.

About one-fifth of the laymen, or 21.7 per cent said that their pastors were often in the community. Seven of these were members of churches having resident pastors. Five laymen with mild sarcasm stated that they saw their pastors frequently around conference time or just before pastors' Anniversaries.

Attitudes of Laymen toward Pastoral Visiting

Although three-fourths of the laymen were aware that their pastors did little visiting in the parish, about an equal percentage, 73.3, stated that the pastor was in the community enough for their needs.

They gave no indication of dissatisfaction with the small amount of pastoral attention. From the church's point of view, these positive answers had negative implications. They indicated:

1. That at the present time, most laymen, 73.3 per cent, see little for the pastor to do in the rural field. On no other basis would such little time be regarded as sufficient time spent in the parish.

2. That most laymen regard the pastoral function chiefly as preaching, and look to the pastorate for little service beyond that (see below).

This restricted view of the pastoral office does not speak well for the rural ministry. It means (1) that the church is not regarded as an important adviser or an integral element in many of the basic aspects of the life of the people. Other agencies and institutions are doing the advising, guiding, or serving.

It also means (2) that as the laity come to depend upon the church less, they may tend to respect the church less (see Chapter Six).

One layman in Calhoun County, when asked if he would like to have a resident pastor, replied, "What would he do around here all the time?" He had no conception of ministerial activity other than preaching. Since a pastor could not preach all day every day, the layman felt he would be idle most of the days, and he feared what an idle mind and idle hands might get into. When told some of the activities that a minister could undertake as means of promoting the social as well as the spiritual welfare of the people, he was surprised to hear that such projects were ever sponsored by ministers, and he was certain they could not be undertaken in his community.

About one-fourth of the laymen felt that pastors are not in their parishes enough, and that they ought to be in them more. One of these was a school principal who had organized a cooperative land purchasing project that he hoped would serve to rebuild the community. He stated that the great need in his community was a minister who could inspire the people to work for their own advancement. He complained that the ministers who were sent to pastor his church were either indifferent or openly hostile to proposals that they assist in plans for community betterment. There was the additional handicap that none of them had sufficient technical training to be of much assistance.

In order to understand something of the nature of the pastor's influence in the rural community, the laymen were asked if they consulted their pastors on ten basic life interests. It was felt that this would show the minister's influence in shaping the daily life of the people. The ten interests were:

work (finding work and adjusting difficulties)
the securing of loans (both personal and farm)
farming methods
marketing of produce
home improvement
schooling of children
problems in rearing children
health
legal troubles
race troubles

The answers of the laymen were predominantly negative. A little more than one-fourth, said that they spoke to their pastors about problems connected with their work. One-sixth consulted pastors on loans, a matter of utmost importance to tenants and renters, and an area in which an interested pastor could probably render considerable service by securing fair rates as well as fair settlements. One-tenth asked advice about farming or marketing problems, and less than one-tenth about matters of health.

Strikingly enough, it was in race troubles that the people depended least on the pastor, only 3.3 per cent consulting him here. Yet this is the one area where the mediatorial services of a good-will leader could be of greatest help to the Negroes involved. The most probable reason why pastors are not consulted in this matter is that they are not on hand when trouble arises. There could also be two other contributory reasons: (1) the pacific, conservative attitude of pastors, already mentioned (Chapter Nine) that could lead people to feel that pastors would not be active in achieving a just settlement; and (2) the fact that many laymen may feel that such matters are not the pastor's field, or that there is little a Negro pastor can do.

Only in problems of rearing children were the ministers consulted by more than half of the persons interviewed, 53.3 per cent. This was generally regarded as a rightful interest of a pastor (a family problem), and parents did not hesitate to consult him in this area. The fact that rural ministers often preach about the sins of the young may serve to give them some authority in this regard.

The extent to which people consulted their pastors varied considerably from county to county. For instance, in Calhoun County only one out of ten laymen consulted the pastor at all, while 90 per cent did not. In Northumberland County approximately one-half of the members looked to their pastors for guidance in the ten interests mentioned.

The Nature of Pastoral Influence

Since a small proportion of members look to their pastors for advice or help in basic issues of life, the ministry therefore plays little part in determining the nature of daily life. In other words, the rural ministry is not widely influential in the more practical but vital aspects of the rural community.

A similar conclusion is reached by V. A. Edwards in a study of Negro leadership in rural Georgia communities.[1] He finds that "from the standpoint of the community's choice of leaders, the farmers rank first, the teachers rank second, the

[1] *Negro Leadership in Rural Georgia Communities,* unpublished Master's thesis, by V. A. Edwards. Cornell University, 1941.

preachers rank third, and the business group holds fourth place."

It is not clear from Mr. Edward's treatment whether the rankings are numerical or qualitative, that is, whether the preachers hold third place because they are fewer than farmers, or because their influence is weaker than that of the farmers. The fact remains, however, that of the persons actually providing leadership in rural Georgia communities, farmers constitute 44 per cent, while preachers constitute 13 per cent. Preachers, therefore, cannot be regarded as the group exercising widest influence in rural communities.

Over against these conclusions is the invariable testimony of persons who work in rural areas, such as teachers, extension workers and health workers, to the effect that the rural pastor *is* influential in the community, so much so that his good will and cooperation must first be obtained if a program in the community is to succeed. For example, one county agent, in speaking of the minister in a community in which he, the county agent, was trying to set up a program, said, "That man can do more on one Sunday to tear down my program than I can build up in thirty days." This was not a thoughtless opinion. It was the result of considerable trouble the agent had experienced in his work.

What then is the nature of the pastor's influence, and upon what does it depend? On the basis of observations made during this study and an experience in rural work extending over twelve years, several conclusions seem trustworthy:

1. The rural pastor is highly influential as a molder of general attitudes, that is, in making his people either favorable or unfavorable toward an issue.

2. He can do this quite easily on certain issues. Tenant status tends to breed a sense of hopelessness and lack of faith, especially in the tenant's ability to work out his own problems. Regarding constructive activities, the people are already indifferent and suspicious. Any disparaging word from the pastor simply confirms and sanctions prejudices already existing in their minds. This is one source of the pastor's ready power in shaping uncooperative attitudes.

3. The rural minister's power as a molder of opinion is not as great on some issues as on others. In many communities there are subjects that pastors dare not touch. Chief of these are sexual behavior, drinking, and certain phases of race relations.

4. The church is still the predominant institution in the rural South. It is the Negro's chief agency of social expression, and it enjoys greater freedom than any other community institution. The pastor as leader of the most important institution commands a unique authority, in spite of his limitations, that no other community leader enjoys.

5. Rural ministers in general are more on the level of the people than other rural workers. Their education is about the same as that of most members, and they are on the same social and economic level. For these reasons they are closer to the people and speak their language more than any other leader. Being more closely identified in some ways, they enjoy an intimacy and a popularity that few other leaders attain. To be sure, the ministers do not live among their people, but, as a rule, neither do any other leaders.

6. Many rural church members, especially the older ones, have great respect for religion and consequently for the re-

ligious leader. In a choice between the pastor and some other leader, they respect the pastor more.

The reasons given by the laymen for not consulting their pastors invariably were: (1) "It is not his business," "not his field," "not a pastor's work," "He is not concerned with these things;" or (2) "He is not here to be consulted."

Since the people do not go to their pastors, they do go to others for the guidance that they need. As might be expected, these others are, in the order of frequency:

> landlord
> neighbors
> friends
> teachers
> doctor
> "government people" (Extension workers)
> business men

Grounds of Church Loyalty

It is evident that the rural Christian is deeply loyal to his pastor and to his church. On no other basis could an untrained, absentee leader hold strong influence over his people. An effort was made to determine the ground of this loyalty. The laymen were asked first, "What benefits do you derive from church membership?" The answers in the order of frequency were:

It helps my soul.

It feeds my soul.

It keeps me straight.

It helps me to be a better Christian.

It lifts me up.

It gives me a chance to work with my brethren.

It gives me spiritual strength.

I get salvation.

Secondly they were asked, "Do you get any benefits from church membership other than religious benefits?" Twenty-three replied that they got an opportunity for fellowship, or, as one rural teacher expressed it, "a chance for social expression;" two said they got help in being better citizens; one said he got help in life problems, and one that he got better character. Thirty-three stated that they got no positive benefits other than religious ones.

It was seen in the interviews that practically all of the lay-men had never thought that other than spiritual benefits should be derived from church membership. They were loyal out of a sense of duty. One deacon spoke for many when he said,

"It's your Christian duty to belong to the church whether you get anything out of it or not."

Being loyal to the church without hope of reward may be blind loyalty, but it is high loyalty, and it is the kind of loyalty the Christian church greatly needs just now. The rural ministry should never abuse it, and American Protestantism should move to see that it is conserved intact.

Summary

Rural Christians do not consult their pastors about practical phases of life, chiefly because they do not know that pastors should be concerned with practical affairs. This lack of pastoral guidance means lack of pastoral influence in the daily life of the people.

While it may fairly be contended that it is not the ministry's duty to market products or to operate farms, it is the church's duty to say when marketing and farming are done according to moral principles and in such ways that they are not destructive of wholesome life or Christian ideals. It is also the duty of the church to see that its people not only believe the Christian gospel but live it. In none of this can a minister serve unless he knows, and unless he is on the scene long enough to serve his people.

At the present time the rural pastor enjoys a unique and strong influence in the rural community. This influence does not rest upon his service or his leadership in the practical affairs of his people. It rests largely upon the Negro's peculiar position in the South, that makes the church the most essential organization and the head of the church the most familiar and intimate leader. The minister's influence rests, too, upon the deep respect that the country Christian has for his religion and his pastor.

Today, however, the pastor finds himself the only untrained leader in the rural community. Teachers, extension workers, nurses are all persons of academic and technical preparation. Gradually the rural people, especially the younger ones, are coming to work with these secular leaders, and to appreciate the services they have to offer. Unless the minister brings to his profession equal preparation, it is quite likely that he will suffer by comparison, losing the place of leadership that at present he happens to hold.

Chapter Twelve

A TRAINED MINISTRY—A GREATER CHURCH

The rural church, like every church, consists of two essential elements: a people joined together in the effort to live the Christian life, and a minister to lead the group in this endeavor. These two together, pastor and people, constitute a church. Both are mutually responsible for the church's greatness or the church's weakness. Both determine whatever progress the church shall be able to make.

This study began in an effort to determine the church's adequacy, that is, the extent to which the rural Negro church is meeting the life-needs of its people. It ends by considering how the inadequacies may be corrected.

The study has revealed a great many deficiencies in rural ministerial service. It has also shown that most of them are directly traceable to two basic causes: (1) the untrained minister and (2) the absentee minister.

A Trained Rural Ministry

The rural ministry lacks academic training, of course, but it also lacks specific knowledge and techniques needed for effective service in rural sections. Further, any attempt at corrective training must be divided into two distinct types: training for theological students, and training for ministers already in service.

Training for Theological Students

In 1940 in the United States there were thirty-two recognized theological seminaries or theological departments for Negroes.[1] Two of the seminaries were accredited by the American Association of Theological Schools. Four seminaries or departments were in institutions that had A ratings (for Negro schools), and six were in schools with B ratings. In other words, only two Negro seminaries out of thirty-two are recognized as having adequate faculty and facilities for giving standard theological training. Four other seminaries or departments are in A grade Negro institutions, but evidently the work of the theological divisions is not sufficient to justify accreditation by the American Association of Theological Schools. Only six of the remaining seminaries or departments are connected with B schools; twenty are in schools that are without accreditation. Thus, as far as theological education in Negro schools is concerned, only 18.8 per cent of it can be thought of as first class. The remaining 81.2 per cent varies from fair to very poor.

In 1944 there were sixty-one Negro students enrolled as undergraduates in sixteen Northern (white) seminaries. All of these seminaries were accredited. If the eighty-two undergraduates in the two accredited Negro seminaries are added,

[1] *Christian Higher Education, A Handbook for 1940,* by Gould Wickey and Ruth E. Anderson, pp. 242-269. Washington, D. C., Council of Church Boards of Education, 1940.

then there were 143 Negro theological students in America who were receiving standardized theological instruction in 1944. Twenty-one of the larger Negro theological schools or departments had 110 graduates in 1944, and the sixteen Northern seminaries had thirteen. Thus something over 123 trained ministers were graduated from the good and poor schools in the past year. There is reason to conclude, however, that very little of this training is such as to prepare men for service in rural areas.

Prior to 1945, none of the Negro theological schools had a rural church department. In response to inquiry, eight Negro schools indicated that they offer a semester course in rural church work, but in six of these the courses were not being given in 1944-45. In neither of the two accredited Negro seminaries was any rural work being offered at the time of the study.

It has been seen (Chapter One) that the Negro church in the South is predominantly rural. Twenty-five of the thirty-two Negro theological schools are located in the South. It would seem that Negro theological education would be concerned to prepare students for the great need at its very door. Yet, to repeat, no Negro Seminary has given major emphasis to rural preparation, and as far as could be learned, fewer than a fourth of them consider the rural field at all.

The lack of interest in rural training is due to the fact that Negro theological education is patterned closely after white theological training. Only in very recent years have the white seminaries awakened to the fact that the rural field is one requiring specialized preparation. Drew University was one of the first to recognize the need and to offer work in this field. In the past ten years other institutions have become interested. At the present time rural church departments are to be found in Boston University School of Theology, Garrett, Drew, Duke, Yale, Andover-Newton, Dubuque and Louisville Seminaries. Iowa State, the University of Illinois, and Cornell cooperate with seminaries in training students. With the exception of the course at Drew, however, the rural work offered in the Northern seminaries is not yet of such calibre as to constitute a major field.

In patterning so closely after traditional methods, the Negro seminaries have missed an opportunity to make a significant contribution to theological education in America. Located in the South, in the heart of a church problem area, if the Negro schools had concentrated on needs that were near, they could have worked out methods and philosophies that would be effective in their immediate areas, and that would have set a pattern for national theological education. The selection of one area of specialized training would have permitted small schools of limited resources to do thorough, creative work. It would have saved Negro theological training from becoming the educational travesty it so often becomes in the poorer schools. For example, the "Dean" of a "seminary" whose physical plant consists of one two-story, four-room, wooden building (in need of repair), whose "faculty" is two persons with bachelor's degrees, and whose "library" is 375 books (many obsolete or worthless)—this "Dean" when questioned about the organization of his curriculum said, "We get catalogs from Boston University, Yale, Drew, Howard, and other schools, and put in as many of these courses as our curriculum will hold. In this way we keep abreast of what the best schools are doing." This "seminary" is located in a state whose Negro population is more than three-fourths rural.

The Phelps-Stokes—Home Missions Council Plan

The most hopeful step yet to be taken in the training of Negro theological students for rural service is the Program for a Better Trained Rural Ministry, sponsored by the Phelps-Stokes Fund of New York City in cooperation with the Home Missions Council. The program is financed by grants from a philanthropic agency. The immediate objectives of the program in undergraduate theological training are:

1. The establishment of rural church departments in ten central Negro seminaries or universities. Financial assistance is given the schools in setting up the departments.

2. Preparing teachers or heads for these departments by giving them at least one year of graduate training beyond the Bachelor of Divinity degree, in rural sociology and agricultural knowledge. (The departments are now in operation.)

3. Recruiting students to take the training that is offered in the ten schools.

In general, the training given the student pastors will have a dual emphasis. It will include basic theological training and also study in rural sociology and basic agricultural skills. The students will learn something of rural community institutions, rural social and economic forces, and of the organization and management of cooperative enterprises.

To be sure, the task of finding enough young men to undertake the necessary training will prove an enormous one, but there is reason to believe that Negro youth will respond to a need when the need is known.

Training for Ministers in Service

There are and there have been a number of activities that aim to help the Negro rural minister now in the field. First among them are the ministerial institutes conducted by schools throughout the South. Some of the schools are private institutions, such as Hampton and Tuskegee Institutes; other are church-related institutions such as the Methodist Negro Ministers' Conference at Gulfside, Mississippi, or the Bishop College Institute, in Marshall, Texas. These institutes, or conferences as they are sometimes called, are held generally in the summer, and last from one to two weeks.

Lectures and courses of study are given. Attendance varies from 50 to 600 (Hampton). The limitations of the institutes are that the instruction period is short, and the larger institutes tend to take on the atmosphere of a social gathering; the work is fragmentary and not systematic or continuous. Certificates of attendance are usually given to those who meet certain requirements.

A second helpful endeavor is the ministerial class, conducted at schools for a part or the whole of the academic year. These classes are of two types. First, there are those that are conducted on the school grounds. Classes conducted at Tuskegee Institute in Alabama and Holsey Institute at Cordele, Georgia, are examples of this type. The Tuskegee class meets each Wednesday throughout the school year. At Holsey Institute the class meets on Thursday and Friday, the ministers staying overnight. The work in both schools is chiefly practical. Courses in reading, writing, grammar, sermon preparation and delivery, church management, and rural community problems

[183]

constitute the bulk of the work. An average enrollment at Tuskegee is thirty-five. In 1944 the enrollment at Cordele was seventy.

The highly varied and limited educational backgrounds of the ministers makes it difficult to set academic standards or to give credit. However, efforts are now being made to work out standardized courses so that academic credit may be given.

In addition to classes held at the schools, there are the classes conducted at outside points by members of the school faculties. These are generally known as extension classes. They are well illustrated in the work of Shaw University in Raleigh, North Carolina. The faculty of the university's Department of Religious Promotion make regular trips to appointed towns within a radius of a hundred miles, where they meet groups of ministers from the surrounding areas. Courses of study are given that run through the year. Some of this work is of sufficient quality to merit academic credit.

While the institutes and classes are helpful to ministers in general, they are not intended primarily for the rural minister. The most specific and the most effective work with rural pastors has been done in the institutes conducted by the Home Missions Council. This agency, representing most of the major Protestant denominations in America, in 1945 held fifty-nine rural pastors' institutes in various parts of the South with a total attendance of 2,123. Most of the institutes were held in cooperation with state and private schools, especially the vocational and agricultural schools.

The Home Missions Council institutes are intended solely for rural people. Those who attend are chosen carefully, and are assisted financially by scholarships. The institutes are conducted by trained directors, regional specialists in rural sociology and religion, each of whom is working in the South through a cooperative arrangement between the Home Missions Council and some state or private school.

These institutes overcome many of the deficiencies of those that are independently sponsored. They are planned by a nation-wide agency that gives them a common emphasis and uniform methods. Their work is standardized, systematized, and directed to the needs of rural areas. In the beginning they were planned for one week. They are now being extended to two or three and even six weeks.

At present eight of the Negro religious extension workers mentioned above are working in seven Southern states. Their specific duty is to work with pastors and people in rural communities. They plan and conduct most of the institutes. Under their direction institutes are held for rural church women as well as for pastors. Twenty-eight of these women's institutes were held in 1945 with a total attendance of 1,201.

The Resident Pastor

As has been mentioned the second great cause of rural ministerial deficiency is the absentee pastor. Obviously little leadership can be given by a minister who is away from his people most of the time. Equally obvious is the cure, a pastor living with and working with his people. Yet to have the cure will require considerable rethinking on the part of individual Christians and national church bodies alike.

The chief requirement for a minister who is to live in a rural parish is an adequate income. This study has shown that while the Negro rural minister is better paid than some other rural workers, particularly the rural teacher, he still is not paid enough to maintain an acceptable standard of living. There are three ways in which the income of rural ministers may be increased: (1) through denominational subsidy; (2) through voluntary salary sharing such as the minimum salary plan now followed in many Methodist conferences and in some other denominations, a plan in which salaries of the higher paid are voluntarily reduced to raise the salaries of the lower paid; and (3) by having the pastor engage in supplementary work.

The first of these, denominational subsidy, is practiced by some of the Negro Methodist groups. But the amounts given are so small that they are actually inconsequential. The second method, voluntary salary equalizing, is not in use in any body of Negro ministers, and if an opinion may be hazarded, is not likely to come soon. The third method is at present the chief one open to the resident rural Negro pastor. This is to find some kind of work with which to supplement his income.

Two activities are readily open to the resident rural pastor: (1) teaching in a rural public school, and (2) farming on a part time basis. Both are quite in keeping with the rural pastorate, and, indeed, may be carried on simultaneously.

In this study, one resident rural pastor was found who was both teacher and pastor. His income from the two occupations was $3,100 per year. In the same county two other resident pastors engaged in farming. Both stated that their annual income from preaching and farming was somewhat above $2,400 per year. None indicated any conflict between preaching and farming or teaching. Those who farmed found it a common bond with their people. The one who taught felt that it gave him an intimate contact with the children of his community that he could get in no other way.

Throughout this study, wherever resident pastors of ability supplemented their preaching by farming, it was found that they enjoyed comfortable incomes as well as intimate contacts with their people. If these men had been trained, they probably could have been effective factors in their communities. Also, the lack of training is perhaps the reason why so few rural ministers teach.

The point here is that where a rural minister is trained either for farming or teaching or some other activity compatible with preaching, he can make a living in the country that will be adequate, and may even exceed that of many city pastors of similar-sized churches. One minister in Virginia, a Negro rural pastor, had an income of over $7,000 per year that he made wholly in his church community. He was a preacher, teacher, and farmer, and excellent at all three. The automobile and good roads are greatly reducing the former hardships of rural living, so that country life can well be as comfortable as life in a town.

Recapitulation

The leadership afforded by the Negro rural ministry is inadequate. This situation can be traced largely to two basic causes: (1) the untrained minister, and (2) the absentee pastorate.

Up to the present time there has been little effort to prepare men for service in the Negro rural church. Negro seminaries, although located in the heart of the rural South, have patterned their instruction after white institutions and have ignored the problem at hand. Until recently white seminaries, with one or two exceptions, have not regarded the rural field as one requiring special training. A few seminaries have awakened to the need, and now offer some instruction, but at present it is not a major field, and the comparatively few Negroes who attend white Seminaries have little chance to get the rural training needed for service in the rural church. Thus practically nothing is being done in theological education to prepare men for genuinely constructive service in rural pastorates.

Something is being done for the Negro rural pastor already in service. The institutes that are being sponsored by secular and church institutions and the extension classes offer some aid.

Most promising both for theological and in-service training is the Program for a Better Trained Rural Ministry, now being developed by the Phelps-Stokes Fund and the Home Missions Council. Through rural church departments in seminaries, and standardized institutes throughout the South, much will be done to lift the level of the rural pastorate. The training under the program will include study in basic agricultural knowledge and rural sociology, as well as sound theological education. This will lead to the well rounded rural ministry.

As to the second great need, the resident pastorate, the chief barrier, fear of insufficient income, need not stand against those who aspire to serve if they are prepared to carry on a supplementary activity, most fittting of which are farming or teaching. Neither of these will take the minister out of the church community.

Denominational Responsibility

Whenever a trained minister leads a Negro rural church, he is an asset to the denomination to which the church belongs. Getting such men into churches is therefore a denominational responsibility. Even so ambitious a plan as the Phelps-Stokes—Home Missions Council Program cannot work without most intimate cooperation by national church bodies. Finding and inspiring men to take the training the program offers is a denominational responsibility.

Above all, denominations can help in rural areas by setting standards. They can refuse to accept men into the rural ministry who do not have adequate preparation, and can require or strongly urge present ministers to improve themselves as rapidly as possible. Every advancement in ministerial efficiency is a gain for the group to which the minister belongs.

National Responsibility

In the foreword to this study it was said that the rural Negro church is a fragment, a part, of the great American Christian body. Any weakness in the part is necessarily a weakness in the whole. The two and three-quarter million colored Christians in the rural South are a significant segment of the American Christian body. Any weakness here is a national problem. The national church cannot afford to be indifferent to the plight of these people.

At the present time the rural Negro's religious life is shot through with deficiencies, chief and most causative of which is the untrained minister. It would appear to be the duty of every first class training agency in the country to recruit and to train leaders for this needy field. Again, the pioneering efforts of Drew Seminary in this regard appear most worthy of emulation.

The Church at the Center

This study has been moved throughout by two convictions, the first of which is that in spite of difficulties of agriculture and race and politics and all the rest, the rural Negro minister can lift the life of his people if he has proper training and is dedicated to the task. The conviction is based upon the fact that some rural ministers have done it.

An excellent example may be seen in the work of a minister in Virginia. A college graduate and a seminary student, twenty-five years ago he refused a call to a city church to take two small churches near a country town. When he went into the community, only two of his members owned their homes. He preached about it, he counseled about it; then set an example by buying his own. Today all the families in his two churches own their homes, most of them bought through his encouragement and advice.

When he went into the community, the little Negro school house was in shameful disrepair. When his appeal to the county education authorities for better facilities was turned down, he led the people of his church in repairing the school building and adding a room. Two years later the county board had been won to sympathy, and voluntarily erected a better school. Today the colored school building is the best in the county, and the minister has served as principal of the school for more than twenty years.

A few years ago, when the school board would not provide

buses for colored children, he purchased buses with funds of his own. Today there is an excellent bus system for colored school children operated by the county.

When he went into the community all of his people grew vegetables for their own tables, but none raised them as cash crops. He first preached about it, but getting no response, he began to raise them himself. Seeing the possibilities, members followed, and today most members raise truck crops for cash. He also introduced poultry raising as a source of supplementary income.

His guidance of young people has been remarkable. Through the years he can count many a man or woman whose life he has had large part in shaping. Many a family has been helped by his kindly, intimate leadership.

To summarize, when this minister entered his rural community, it was typical of Negro rural communities in the South. Today, through the labor of a devoted rural Negro ministerial leader, the community is one of the most outstanding in the nation as far as Negro welfare is concerned. Through it all he has not suffered financially. He is the minister mentioned above whose income exceeded $7,000 a year. He stands as an indication of what a trained, consecrated man can do.

The second conviction that permeates this work is that the church is or should be the central, indeed the centripetal force around which the life of a community should move. This conviction is held because the church is the one agency in a community that aspires to touch the whole of life, and, whether it wishes it or not, is held responsible for every area of life. For example, no one would think of blaming the rural school for rotten rural politics. No one would blame a county agent for immoral conditions in a home. But the church is blamed for both these and more. The church is held responsible because the church is concerned with right and wrong in every aspect of human living.

If the church is to assume responsibility for the many areas of life, it must have a ministry capable of giving spiritual direction in the many areas of life. There are two ways in which this direction can be given. One is by verbal admonition, that is, by sermons. The other is by intimate, constant leadership in the affairs of the daily routine. Of the first type, that is, of sermons, the rural Negro church seems to have had somewhat more than its share. Of the second type it has had very little indeed.

The spiritual direction that the rural colored church community so much needs has implications that far transcend the borders of the backyard colored communities. It is not enough that agricultural workers, or any workers for that matter, shall simply make good wages. It is not enough that rural life, like urban life, shall be filled with creature comforts. A civilization is only strong when its drives are in conformity with the will of God. A nation can long endure only when the personal self-interest of every citizen is subordinated to the needs of the common human brotherhood that Christianity proclaims. Every minister in a rural community who gives practical spiritual direction to the people he serves is not only helping the people of his community, but is working to make this nation strong.

Twenty years ago a man who has devoted his life to the rural church wrote a prophetic passage:

The day is coming, we believe, when every hill and valley will re-echo the music of the church bell; when every field and farm will feel the touch of Christian husbandmen; when the farm markets will be peopled by men who do justice and love mercy; when every highway shall lead to a place of worship; when men's hearts will be full of love for their neighbors; when children will be taught righteousness by devoted and trained teachers; when the nation will recognize the value of the rural church to our national idealism; when ministers will be proud to serve rural parishes; when those who worship in city centers will seek the companionship of rural folk because of their real worth.[1]

These words can still serve as the ideal for the rural church today.

[1] *Our Templed Hills,* by Ralph A. Felton, pp. ix-x. New York, Council of Women for Home Missions and Missionary Movement, 1926. Used by permission.

A SELECTED READING LIST

THE FOLLOWING reading list, while not devoted exclusively to the rural Negro church, will afford (I) insights into the history of the church among Negroes in America and (II) a picture of the rural South as the setting of the Negro church in that section. Books, magazine articles, and unpublished manuscripts are included. Some of the books listed are now out of print, but are still available in public and private libraries for reference work.

I. Christian Beginnings and Development

Brooks, Walter H., "The Evolution of the Negro Baptist Church." *Journal of Negro History*, 7:11-22; January, 1922.

Daniel, W. A., THE EDUCATION OF NEGRO MINISTERS. New York, George H. Doran Co., 1925.

Davis, Allison, "Negro Churches and Associations in the Lower South." Unpublished manuscript (in the Schomburg Collection, Harlem Branch, New York Public Library).

Du Bois, W. E. B., BLACK RECONSTRUCTION. New York, Harcourt, Brace and Co., 1935.

Du Bois, W. E. B., "Religion of Negroes." *New World*, 9:614, 1900.

Du Bois, W. E. B., THE NEGRO CHURCH. Atlanta, Ga., Atlanta University Press, 1903; viii. 212 pp.

Earnest, Joseph B., THE RELIGIOUS DEVELOPMENT OF THE NEGRO IN VIRGINIA. Charlottesville, Virginia, Michie Co., 1914; 233 pp.

Fry, C. Luther, THE U. S. LOOKS AT ITS CHURCHES. Institute of Social and Religious Research, 1930.

Harrison, W. P., THE GOSPEL AMONG THE SLAVES. Nashville, Tennessee; Publishing House, M. E. Church, South, 1893.

Herskovitz, Melville J., THE MYTH OF THE NEGRO PAST. New York, Harper and Brothers, 1944.

Imes, G. Lake, "Negro Ministers and Country Life." *Religious Education*, 7:169-75; June, 1912.

Jernegan, Marcus Wilson, SLAVERY AND CONVERSION IN THE AMERICAN COLONIES. New York, The Macmillan Co., 1916. Reprinted from *American Historical Review*, vol. XXI, no. 3; April, 1916.

Johnson, Guion G. and Guy B. Johnson, "The Church and the Race Problem in the United States." Unpublished manuscript, 1940 (in the Schomburg Collection, Harlem Branch, New York Public Library).

Jones, Charles Colcock, Jr., THE RELIGIOUS INSTRUCTION OF THE NEGROES IN THE UNITED STATES. Savannah, Ga., T. Purse, 1842; xxii, 227 pp.

JOURNAL OF REV. FRANCIS ASBURY. New York, Lane and Scott, 1852. 3 volumes.

Mays, Benjamin E., "The Negro Church in American Life." *Christendom*, an ecumenical review, vol. 5, no. 3; Summer, 1940; pp. 387-398.

Mays, Benjamin E., THE NEGRO'S GOD AS REFLECTED IN HIS LITERATURE. Boston, Chapman and Grimes, Inc., 1938.

Mays, Benjamin E., and Joseph W. Nicholson, THE NEGRO'S CHURCH. New York, Institute of Social and Religious Research, 1933.

Pierre, C. E., "The Work of the Society for the Propagation of the Gospel in Foreign Parts among Negroes of the Colonies." *Journal of Negro History*, 1:349-60; October, 1916.

Pitman, F. W., "Fetishism, Witchcraft, and Christianity among the Slaves." *Journal of Negro History*, 11:650-68; October, 1926.

Raymond, Charles A., "The Religious Life of the Negro Slave." *Harper's Monthly*, 27:479-88, 676-82, 816-25, 1863.

Sweet, William H., "Negro Churches in the South; a Phase of Reconstruction." *Methodist Review*, 104-405-18; May, 1921.

Washington, Booker Taliaferro, "The Religious Life of the Negro." *North American Review*, 181:20-3; July, 1905.

Wilson, G. R., "The Religion of the American Negro Slave: His Attitude toward Life and Death." *Journal of Negro History,* 7:41-27; January, 1923.

Wish, Harvey, "American Slave Insurrections before 1861." *Journal of Negro History,* vol. 22, no. 3; July, 1937; pp. 299-320.

Woodson, Carter G., THE HISTORY OF THE NEGRO CHURCH. Washington, D. C., The Associated Publishers, 1921.

II.   *The Race Problem and the Southern Scene*

Davis, Allison and John Dollard, CHILDREN OF BONDAGE. Washington, D. C., American Council on Education, 1940.

Davis, John W., "George Liele and Andrew Byran, Pioneer Negro Baptist Preachers." *Journal of Negro History,* 3:119-27; April, 1918.

Dollard, John, CASTE AND CLASS IN A SOUTHERN TOWN. New Haven, Yale University Press, 1937.

Duggan, I. W., "Cotton, Land and People: A Statement of the Problem." *Journal of Farm Economics,* vol. 22, no. 1; February, 1940; pp. 188-197.

Edwards, V. A., "Negro Leadership in Rural Georgia Communities." Unpublished master's thesis, Cornell University, 1941.

Johnson, Charles S., GROWING UP IN THE BLACK BELT: NEGRO YOUTH IN THE RURAL SOUTH. Washington, D. C., American Council on Education, 1941.

Johnson, Charles S., PATTERNS OF NEGRO SEGREGATION. New York, Harper and Brothers, 1943.

Johnson, Charles S., SHADOW OF THE PLANTATION. Chicago, The University of Chicago Press, 1934.

Johnson, Charles S., Edwin R. Embree, and W. W. Alexander, THE COLLAPSE OF COTTON TENANCY. Chapel Hill, The University of North Carolina Press, 1945.

Kennedy, Louise Venable, THE NEGRO PEASANT TURNS CITYWARD. New York, Columbia University Press, 1930.

Kester, Howard, REVOLT AMONG THE SHARECROPPERS. New York, Covici, Friede, 1936.

Morse, W. H., "Lemuel Haynes." *Journal of Negro History,* 4:22-32; January, 1919.

Myrdal, Gunnar, AN AMERICAN DILEMMA. New York, Harper and Brothers, 1944. 3 volumes.

Olmsted, Frederick L., THE COTTON KINGDOM: A TRAVELER'S OBSERVATIONS ON COTTON AND SLAVERY IN THE AMERICAN SLAVE STATES. New York, Mason Brothers, 1861-1862. 2 volumes.

Raper, Arthur F., PREFACE TO PEASANTRY: A TALE OF TWO BLACK BELT COUNTIES. Chapel Hill, The University of North Carolina Press, 1936.

Raper, Arthur F., and Ira de A. Reid, SHARECROPPERS ALL. Chapel Hill, The University of North Carolina Press, 1941.

Raper, Arthur F., THE TRAGEDY OF LYNCHING. Chapel Hill, The University of North Carolina Press, 1933.

Stephens, Oren, "Revolt on the Delta." *Harper's Magazine,* vol. 183, no. 1,098; November, 1941; pp. 656-664.

Sterner, Richard, and others, THE NEGRO'S SHARE. New York, Harper and Brothers, 1943.

Thompson, Edgar T., "Population Expansion and the Plantation System." *The American Journal of Sociology,* vol. 41, no. 3; November, 1935; pp. 314-326.

Thompson, Edgar T., ed., RACE RELATIONS AND THE RACE PROBLEM. Durham, N. C., Duke University Press. 1939.

Vance, Rupert B., HUMAN FACTORS IN COTTON CULTURE: A STUDY IN THE SOCIAL GEOGRAPHY OF THE AMERICAN SOUTH. Chapel Hill, The University of North Carolina Press, 1929.

Vance, Rupert B., COTTON AND TENANCY. Dallas, Texas, Southern Regional Committee, Social Science Research Council, 1936.

Wayman, A. W., MY RECOLLECTIONS OF A. M. E. MINISTERS. Philadelphia, A.M.E. Book Concern, 1881. 250 pp.

Woodson, Carter G., THE RURAL NEGRO. Washington, D. C., Association for the Study of Negro Life and History, 1930.

Woofter, T. J., Jr., LANDLORD AND TENANT ON THE COTTON PLANTATION. Washington, D. C., Works Progress Administration, 1936.

INDEX